Other Books by Gloria Gaither

Because He Lives: The Stories and Inspiration Behind the Songs of Bill and Gloria Gaither

Friends Through Thick and Thin (with Peggy Benson, Sue Buchanan, and Joy MacKenzie)

My Father's Angels

Ordinary Baby, Extraordinary Gift

GOD GAVE THE Song

Glimpses into the Inspiration
Behind the Songs of
Bill and Gloria Gaither

GLORIA GAITHER

ZondervanPublishingHouse

Grand Rapids, Michigan

A Division of HarperCollins*Publishers*

God Gave the Song
Copyright © 2000 by Gloria Gaither

Requests for information should be addressed to:

ZondervanPublishingHouse
Grand Rapids, Michigan 49530

Library of Congress Cataloging-in-Publication Data
Gaither, Gloria.
    God gave the song: glimpses into the inspiration behind the songs of Bill and Gloria Gaither
    / Gloria Gaither.
       p.   cm.
    ISBN: 0-310-23123-X (hardcover : alk. paper)
    1. Gaither, Gloria.   2. Gaither, Bill.   3. Gospel musicians—United States—Biography.
4. Christian biography—United States.   I. Gaither, Gloria. Songs. Texts. Selections.   II. Title.

ML420.G13 A3 2000
782.25'4'0922–dc21
[B]   00-043729

This edition printed on acid-free paper.

Interior design by Melissa Elenbaas
Printed in the United States of America

---

00 01 02 03 04 05 06 /❖ DC/ 10 9 8 7 6 5 4 3 2 1

Contents

Foreword

by Suzanne Gaither Jennings

The first time something I had written was rejected was when I was fourteen years old. I had been writing poems and prose and dabbling in songwriting since I was seven. I had found myself in the center of creative circles my whole life, grew up in a family of songwriters, musicians, and poets, and evidently had some degree of inherent writing and verbal abilities. So in the small farming community in which we lived, my English, literature, and writing teachers seemed glad to have me in their classes, and until I was fourteen, the only other people who had seen or heard any of my "work" were my entirely "unbiased" parents. So I was taken aback when a songwriter friend of our family, whose opinion meant a great deal to me, lovingly offered a negative comment about a song I had written.

Even though I was only fourteen, I had written several songs, but in my humble teenage opinion, this song, titled "You Are the Way," had the best shot of landing on someone's contemporary Christian album. I had written the song — words and music — completely on my own and made a demo of it with a full rhythm section at my father's studio. Confident, I played my song for this family friend one evening when he and his wife had come for supper. After the song came to its boisterous and dramatic conclusion, I smiled at our friend and bravely asked, "So, what do you think?"

I will never forget his response. "I think, Suzanne, that you are writing about themes that are over your head. This isn't *you* talking here."

I was so devastated that it was a while before I gathered enough courage to try again.

In the years following, my work was rejected many more times. The comments varied but always had the same theme. "You're writing beyond your years." "You need to be more honest here." "You can't possibly understand what you're verbalizing." My favorite rejection came from an editor of a well-known Christian book publishing company when my sister, Amy, and I presented her with a collection of poems, a joint effort, for her consideration. She said, "There are some interesting ideas here, but you don't seem to have found your own voice."

After that meeting, I set out on a fervent and sometimes perilous mission to "find my own voice." I began dissecting my writing with a dark, black marker, crossing out anything that smacked of T. S. Eliot or Robert Frost or Billy Joel or Sting. The exercise was laborious and painful, and I began to see more black on my beloved pages than pen markings.

It was not until a few years later when I had "been through" some things in my life that I began to hear "the Song." It happened several times, but I remember one incident in particular. I had been through an unexpected and frightening surgery for a mysterious mass on my ovary shortly before discovering I was pregnant with my son Will. The recuperation and pregnancy were difficult and draining, and we worried about Will's welfare until the day he was born. We were relieved that he seemed to be perfectly healthy, and it wasn't long before I found out I was pregnant with my second son, Jesse. I was hopeful that this pregnancy would be different, but as it progressed, my weakness and sickness turned out to be more pronounced and longer lasting than during the first pregnancy. In that year and the year following Jesse's birth, I fought against my ailing body and was tested for everything from thyroid disorders to M.S. Eventually, and for no apparent reason, my health began to improve; I had come to the end of a three-year physical ordeal.

Driving home one warm summer evening, thinking about my beautiful babies and thanking God for His mercies, I began to hear a string of words in my head.

There's a place for pain in the care of the soul.
To die is gain, so to live is the whole.

And if perspectives change, it's sometimes for the best —
A chance to rearrange, to put faith to the test.[1]

I couldn't get home fast enough. I ran in the door, grabbed a note-book and pen, and plopped into a wicker chair on the screened-in porch. What I wrote was a lyric called "Against the Grain," which became my testimony. I did not care whether it would become the next contempo-rary Christian hit; I didn't even care if it was ever recorded at all. I had heard the Song, and the Song had come to me through suffering and dis-appointment and silence.

In the search for my own voice, I discovered that the Song can never be mine, that I can never possess the Voice I hear, no matter how many awards may line my walls or how many accolades may follow my name. But I also discovered that the more I suffer through, the more discour-agement I weather, the more my soul pants after the Soul of God, the louder the Song gets in my ears, and all I'm required to do is write it down. I wish in all their experience and adult wisdom some of my well-intentioned critics had told me the truth, had looked into my naïve hope-ful eyes and said, "Suzanne, this is not you talking — may it never be you who talks here." Or, "Forget about finding your own voice, but follow the way of the cross, suffer with Him, participate in His silence; then you will find His voice, which, you will discover, is much truer than your own."

May we always continue to be bold enough to leave our own voices behind. May we never forget the One from whom the Song always comes.

God Gave the Song

You ask me why my heart keeps singing,
Why I can sing when things go wrong;
But since I've found the source of music,
I just can't help it; God gave the song.

Come walk with me thru fields and forests;
We'll climb the hills and still hear that song,
For even hills resound with music —
They just can't help it; God gave the song.

Yes, God gave the song. It's always been with us. The song came into our world through a manger — a manger in Bethlehem. It was a simple song — a simple lovely song for every man. Right from the first, some tried to ignore it. They said, "There's no song! It simply doesn't exist." Others just tried to change the tune. They made laws to stop it. Armies marched against it. They killed some who sang the song. They screamed at it in fury; they tried to drown it out. Finally they nailed that song to a tree. They said to themselves, "There . . . that should take care of that!" But it didn't!

What's that I hear? I still hear that music!
Day after day, that song goes on.
For once you know that source of music,
You'll always hear it; God gave the song.

Come on and join! It's the song of Jesus.
Day after day, that song goes on.
For once you know the source of music,
You'll always hear it; God gave the song.

God Gave the Song

by Gloria Gaither

The Song of Life has to be written; there is no better and no other explanation than that. The song dictates its own time and place. It chooses its own circumstances. It grows in daily experience until it just can't stay inside any longer. The writer gets uncomfortable, pregnant with the growing life. It can't be stopped.

It might be after breakfast one morning; it might be late at night. It could be on the tour bus or on an airplane at thirty thousand feet. It could be at the grocery store downtown or at our little cabin in the woods. It could be on vacation at the seashore or on the way to pick up the grandkids from school. But when it's time, Bill and I have found the song *will* come.

Some songs take a midwife. Some require long labor. Other songs pour out so unexpectedly that we are completely unprepared. We find ourselves grabbing whatever instruments are handy: a napkin in a restaurant, a canceled check, a used envelope, the sole of a shoe; a piece of chalk, a stub of a pencil.

So why do we write? How does a song come to be?

Bill and I have found that we just can't help it. It's that simple!

Part One

⊱☙●☙⊰

A heart full of singing starts
with a relationship with God.
From a gnawing hunger somewhere deep in the human spirit
to the realization that the
"something missing" is the One
who made us, spiritual awak-
ening is a process unique to
each individual.

I Just Feel Like Something Good Is about to Happen

I just feel like something good is about to happen!
I just feel like something good is on its way!
God has promised that He'd open all of heaven,
And, brother, it could happen any day.
When God's people humble themselves and call on Jesus,
And they look to heaven expecting as they pray,
I just feel like something good is about to happen,
And, brother, this could be that very day!

I have learned in all that happens just to praise Him,
For I know He's working all things for my good;
Ev'ry tear I shed is worth all the investment,
For I know He'll see me through — He said He would.
He has promised eye nor ear could hardly fathom
All the things He has in store for those who pray;
I just feel like something good is about to happen,
And, brother, this could be that very day!

Yes, I've noticed all the bad news in the paper,
And it seems like things get bleaker ev'ry day;
But for the child of God it makes no diff'rence,
Because it's bound to get better either way.
I have never been more thrilled about tomorrow;
Sunshine's always bursting through the skies of gray.
I just feel like something good is about to happen,
And, brother, this could be that very day!

I Just Feel Like Something Good Is about to Happen

Bill is an optimist. He always thinks things are going to get better, or at least resolved. He believes problems are for solving, mountains are for climbing, and *impossible* isn't a very useful word. I tell him he's like the kid who got a barn full of manure for his birthday and was so excited because he just knew there *had* to be a pony in there somewhere!

Bill can make an adventure out of a convertible ride in the country and a celebration out of the first white Indiana peach to ripen in the orchard.

He's made our children — and now our grandchildren — remember the times they "camped out" under the dining room table spread with a blanket to make a tent more than they remember the trip we took to Paris.

He believes in people and in the treasure of talent he sees buried in them. Even when they disappoint him and sometimes betray him, he always hopes they will learn from their mistakes and believes that God isn't finished with them yet.

Now don't get me wrong. Bill isn't naïve and he doesn't avoid confrontation. He's an old teacher, and although his patience is much longer than mine, eventually, he is not fooled by "shenanigans," as my dad would say. When he feels the time is right, he will bite the bullet and, if he can, use a negative situation as an opportunity to teach, still believing that human resources are the most valuable creation of God and that they should not be wasted.

Many times in our lives we faced circumstances — business reversals, failures, disappointments — that might have made other men give up and quit. But Bill's nature is not to consider an obstacle a dead end. It might take a detour, but there is always a way. At times like these he always quotes an old football expression: just stay in the pocket.

Someone once asked Chuck Swindoll for the secret of his and Cynthia's incredible ministry — the number of books he has produced, the powerful media impact of their broadcasts. He said something like this: "Well, our main secret is just to show up for work." Bill loved that. Just keep doing what you know to do, and do it with all the energy you have.

There is a wonderful line from a well-known poem by Kipling, titled "If," that says, "If you can meet with triumph and disaster / and treat those two impostors just the same." Bill often quotes that to young people who think they're winning or losing big. "The truth is," he'll say, "you're probably not winning as big as you think you are, and when you fail, you're probably not losing as big as you think you are either." Both great successes and huge failures are impostors in our lives. Real life is the regular days. It is of the ordinary that we must make something magic. And it is embedded in the black coal that diamonds are found.

Scripture is full of soothing and encouraging words; it is full of instruction. But the verses that get quoted most around our house include these:

We know that all things work together for good to them that love God, to them who are called according to his purpose.

ROMANS 8:28 KJV

For I am persuaded, that neither death, nor life, nor angels, nor principalities, nor powers, nor things present, nor things to come, nor height, nor depth, nor any other creature, shall be able to separate us from the love of God, which is in Christ Jesus our Lord.

ROMANS 8:38–39 KJV

Fix your thoughts on what is true and good and right. Think about things that are pure and lovely, and dwell on the fine, good things in others. Think about all you can praise God for and be glad about. Keep putting into practice all you learned . . . and the God of peace will be with you.

PHILIPPIANS 4:8–9 LB

Genesis 1 tells us that God saw the light and said it was good. God said the land and the sea were good, the plants and flowers and trees with their fruit and flowers and seeds were good. God said spring and summer, fall and winter were good, the sunshine and stars and moon were good. He said the squirrels and birds, geese and wolves, woodchucks and butterflies were good and that it was good they could make babies and reproduce themselves. And then He made people and said they were very good.

God Himself found miraculous delight in things we stumble over every day and never say, "My, how good this is!" Things such as our homes, our children, the peaches and tomatoes, friendships and stars, snapdragons and water, bumblebees and business associates. Bill is right! In all that, if we stay in the pocket, show up for work, and love God with all our hearts, something good is bound to happen.

I Heard It First on the Radio

Jesus loves me, this I know,
For the Bible tells me so —
      And I heard it first on the radio.
This love of God so rich and strong
Shall be the saint's and angel's song —
      I heard it first on the radio.
Amazing grace — how sweet the sound —
The lost and lonely can be found,
And grace can even save a wretch like me!
No other love could make a way;
No other love my debts could pay —
      And I heard it first on the radio.

Needing refuge for my soul
When I had no place to go —
      I heard it first on the radio.
From a life of wasted years,
He gave me peace and calmed my fears —
      And I heard it first on the radio.
Had I not heard, where would I be
Without this love that lifted me
When I was lost and nothing else would help?
Just as I was without one plea,
Sweet Jesus came and rescued me —
      And I heard it first on the radio;
      Yes, I heard it first on the radio.

Alas, and did my Savior bleed
That captive spirits could be freed —
      And I heard it first on the radio.

My soul has found a resting place
Until I meet Him face to face —
          And I heard it first on the radio.
I love to tell the story true,
And those who know still love it, too;
Oh, what a precious Friend we have in Him!
And when in glory saints will tell,
'Twill be the theme they love so well —
          And we heard it first on the radio.

I Heard It First on the Radio

~

Bill grew up on a farm in a part of Indiana where the land is flat and the corn, hay, soybean, and wheat fields stretch clear to the horizon. This is the region where the prairie begins, reaching across Illinois and on through Nebraska — part of the breadbasket of the world.

So many Indiana farm boys like Bill grew up learning to bale hay, thresh wheat, and shuck corn — by machine, of course. Many took over their fathers' farms before small farmers were squeezed into oblivion by huge agribusiness investors. Other boys aspired to attend technological schools, hoping to secure management positions in one of the auto-related industries that pumped lifeblood into the Midwestern economy.

Bill, however, was something of a mutation. Allergic to the hay fields and not the least bit mechanically inclined, he spent his Saturdays and after-school hours pretending to broadcast to the neighbors out of the upstairs window of the old farmhouse where he grew up. Mornings and evenings while milking the cows his father raised, he would tune in one of the "clear channel" stations from Nashville, Atlanta, or Memphis on the dust-covered old barn radio. That's where he first heard the rich harmony of the quartets and family groups from the South.

At first it was just the rhythms and the harmonies that captured his heart. But the more he listened, the more the messages began to sink in. The radio became his lifeline to another world, another reality.

Although they didn't completely understand this strange child, his parents encouraged his dreams. When he left for school in the mornings, young William would leave instructions for his mother to record on their wire recorder (the forerunner of the tape recorder) the gospel music radio shows that came on in the afternoon. If a group he loved came on while he was in the fields helping his dad in the summer, his mother would run across the farm to let him know.

Family vacations became trips to hear these groups in person at the Ryman Auditorium in Nashville or the Quartet Convention in Memphis. Never did he miss an opportunity to attend the "singings" at Cadle Tabernacle in Indianapolis when the groups came to Indiana.

Meanwhile, Bill was becoming involved in his local church and teaching his little sister and younger brother to sing harmony. He was learning the words to the songs the best groups sang, words with meaning and content.

Many influences play a part in bringing each of us to a personal encounter with God: pastors, teachers, godly parents, old saints, great writers and communicators who express God's love with passion and compassion. But Bill would probably tell you that the singing groups he heard on the radio were among the most important influences in his young life.

Now hardly a day goes by without our receiving letters and e-mail telling us stories of the part radio played in someone else's conversion, encouragement, healing, or enlightenment. New communications technology emerges every day. But for countless thousands like Bill Gaither, it was, and continues to be, radio that carried the message that changed their lives. Only eternity will reveal how many will be assembled around the great white throne because they "heard it first on the radio."

Come Sunday

On Monday she is teaching school —
On Tuesday he's a cop —
On Wednesday she gives haircuts
      in her small-town beauty shop.
On Thursday he's a businessman —
On Friday he'll plant wheat —
On Saturday she drives a taxi
      through the city streets.

    But come Sunday,
    In a place called Hope —
    Come Sunday,
    They'll put on their robes;
    Come Sunday,
    They'll be singing in the choir —
    Come Sunday,
    God's children all come home.

On Monday she'll be looking for
Some kind of part-time job —
By Wednesday he'll go into town
To sell the summer crop —
And Friday's when the note comes due
For the mortgage on their place —
He knows that Mary's worried;
He can see it in her face.
    But come Sunday . . .

The Mondays of a lifetime here
Will only bring a sigh.
The days, the weeks, the months, the years —

How swiftly they flew by!
The cares of life, the joys we knew —
But faded memories —
When Father calls His children home
To spend eternity.

> *And come Sunday*
> *In a place called Hope —*
> *Come Sunday,*
> *We'll put on our robes;*
> *Come Sunday,*
> *We'll be singing in the choir —*
> *Come Sunday,*
> *God's children will be home.*

Come Sunday

*B*ill and I love to see the choir file in on Sunday morning, all dressed in their robes and singing praises to the Lord. Perhaps we love it so much because we know so many of the people under the robes. There's my friend Kathy, a single mom who recently remarried, struggling to raise two boys and now to blend a family. And there's my brother-in-law Dave, recently retired from engineering at an automobile factory and loving every minute of his freed-up life. And Rod. He's struggling with a debilitating disease that is changing his tall handsome body and threatening to cut short his life. And there's Karen, whom I love like a sister, a woman after God's own heart; we raised teenagers together and meet in a Bible study now every Monday at 7:00 A.M. Behind her in the choir is Randy, a fine choral conductor in his own right who still gets a kick out of singing and making harmony.

All of them agree to lay aside their routines and the demands of the workaday world to focus on the God of the universe — come Sunday. They all have different musical tastes. Some like jazz; some love rock 'n' roll. I know a few enjoy a good ole hoedown, and a couple love opera and the symphony. But come Sunday, they all lay aside their musical preferences to sing a "song unto the Lord."

Beneath those robes are all sorts of bodies. Some are tall and lean; some are round and soft. Some of the choir members work at muscle tone; others are just glad to have bodies at all after birthing twins or surviving cancer or getting through open heart surgery. But come Sunday, they put on their robes, and suddenly they are a unity of singing and praise.

Their incomes and wardrobes are nothing alike. Joe would not be caught dead in a three-piece suit, while Jerry would not be caught without one. Marcy buys most of her clothes at Target, if the truth be known, while the girl next to her has been dressed in designer tags since she was in diapers. But come Sunday ... they're the choir.

All week long we're the family of God. Working, writing, teaching, nursing, governing, administering, mothering, fathering, investing, brokering, learning, studying, driving, clerking — we are members one of the other. But come Sunday, we are the congregation. We are the body of Christ.

> *I, therefore, the prisoner of the Lord, beseech you that ye walk worthy of the vocation wherewith ye are called, with all lowliness and meekness, with longsuffering, forbearing one another in love; Endeavouring to keep the unity of the Spirit in the bond of peace. There is one body, and one Spirit, even as ye are called in one hope of your calling; One Lord, one faith, one baptism, one God and Father of all who is above all, and through all, and in you all.*
>
> *EPHESIANS 4:1–6 KJV*

Come Sunday the choir lifts its voice in praise and reminds us of the Hope we have within us. Come Sunday . . .

Hear the Voice of My Beloved

Hear the voice of my beloved
Gently call at close of day,
"Come, my love; oh, come and meet me.
Rise, oh rise, and come away."

"Winter's dark will soon be over
And the rains are nearly done;
Flowers bloom and trees are budding —
Time for singing has begun."

I have waited through the shadows
For my Lord to call for me.
Now the morning breaks eternal;
In its light, His face I see.
Now the morning breaks eternal,
And at last His face I see.

"When you see the fig tree budding,
You will know the summer's near.
When you hear the words I've spoken,
You will know my coming's near."

"Keep on list'ning, my beloved,
For my coming's very near."

Hear the Voice of My Beloved

Maybe it's because our lives have always been so public. Or maybe it's because I'm a hermit at heart. But the times I treasure most are private, intimate times with those I love. Oh, don't get me wrong. I love a party, and massive "happenings" are fun to plan and a thrill to experience. Bill is the "event" champion of the world. Show him an arena and his mind will go off like a rocket, planning a celebration to fill it. No one can touch him, in my opinion, at putting together an evening, programming talent and making everyone "win." It brings him joy to see artists use their gifts in the best possible setting so that no one is the star but the total experience is life changing for audience and performers alike. It's what he does best.

But when the lights go out and the building is an empty cavern, when the posters are crammed into gray plastic trash bags and the popcorn is swept from the hallways, I long to slip away with Bill someplace where no one knows our name and walk beside the sea or climb through the woods at the top of a cliff or simply walk under the archway of willow bows that weep beside our own creek in a little Indiana town.

I never get enough of times like those, and I can't stop my longing for them. Sometimes I feel selfish. I reprove myself for wanting to leave the throngs and disappear into the desert . . . together, alone.

Many times in our marriage I have felt guilty for wanting Bill to myself. "Ministry" can be a challenging rival. How could I be jealous of "God's work"? Most of the time it was work we chose and did together. Yet just when I felt our love needing nourishment, the schedule was already set, the concert advertised, and the worship planned; I knew in my heart we were going to be ministering out of our own need, not out of our plenty. Those were the times we simply had to admit to ourselves, and to God, our emotional bankruptcy and rely on the knowledge that God's storehouse is always full. Amazingly, we would come away not drained but restored — and we knew the multitudes were fed as well.

We have always loved the Song of Solomon. We love it not just as a metaphor of God's longing for His church, His bride, but as a very passionate and human poem about two lovers who can't get each other off their minds. Even in the marketplace, they search for one fleeting glimpse of the object of their affection. The night breeze carries her perfume to him; the lambs nestled on the hillside remind him of her breasts. Everything she does to make herself beautiful is for him; the sound of footsteps below her window arouses her hope that he is coming to their secret place.

I truly believe that the sweetest of intimacies on earth — the marriage of two lovers — is the nearest we can know of the intimacy God longs for us to experience with Him. On the job, in the street, in the crowds, in the commerce of life, His presence is always hovering on the periphery of our consciousness. He makes no bones about His affection for the beloved of His heart. He is jealous of all other loves — He will have no rivals! And in return He will withhold no good thing — even His own Son — to woo back the affection stolen by lesser gods. When He has our exclusive allegiance, He showers every good and perfect gift on His bride, and He spares no expense to make her perfect and bring her home to His singular presence.

On my finger I wear a ring Bill had made for me of twenty-four-carat gold in the land where the Song of Solomon was written. On it is an inscription I will never be able to resist. I don't hear it often enough, and I can't get enough of it. "Arise, my love and come away" (Song 2:13 KJV), it says in Hebrew. I will arise, my Lord, and come.

More of You

I'm not trying to find just some new frame of mind
That will change my old point of view,
For I've been through it all;
Deep inside nothing's changed — I'm not new.
I'm not seeking a gift or emotional lift,
But one thing I'm longing to do
Is to lift up my cup and let You fill it up with just You.

> More of You, more of You —
> I've had all, but what I need
> Just more of You.
> Of things I've had my fill
> And yet I hunger still;
> Empty and bare,
> Lord, hear my prayer
> For more of You.

I have searched all around in the husks that abound,
But I find no nourishment there;
Now my strength's almost gone
And I feel the pull of despair;
Yet my thirst drives me on and I stumble along
Over ground so barren and dry;
For the spring's just ahead — Living Water! "Lord, fill me," I cry.

> More of You, more of You —
> I've had all, but what I need
> Just more of You.
> Of things I've had my fill
> And yet I hunger still;
> Empty and bare,
> Lord, hear my prayer
> For more of You.

More of You

Most people believe in God. The very limitations of humanity direct our hopes toward the existence of some higher power. The workings of the tiniest organism, the detail of each leaf and flower, the order of the universe, the wonder of the oceans teeming with sea life, the marvel of a newborn — these call to all that is rational in us to believe that a master intelligence is behind it all. The metaphysical knowing that something transcends us draws us like a magnet to an awareness of "soul" and of a place beyond the grave and of life beyond the final breath. Historical record and modern surveys confirm that most people in most cultures believe in some kind of God.

But can we know this God? Can there be any relationship with this Being beyond being? What would be required of the human creature to build a bridge to such an awesome Creator? This is the ancient question. That we be granted an audience and then have a relationship with such a power would surely require something great of us. What would make this Being, this Mastermind, pay attention? What would please or anger?

Speculations about the answer to these questions have given birth to all manner of superstitions and incredible behaviors. Babies have been thrown into rivers or burned on sacrificial pyres. Bodies have been carved and mutilated, crops and livestock have been offered, images have been constructed of iron, stone, gold, silver, and wood. Buildings have been erected and decorated. Pilgrimages have been taken. Feasting and fasting, indulgence and deprivation, wild celebrations and austere withdrawal into hermitage have all been practiced in the devout belief that these might bring this God into contact with mortals and thus bring some answers to the mystery of life.

We who call ourselves Christians believe that we could never bridge this great chasm but that this great God instead chose to come to us. What a revolutionary idea! And beyond that, we believe that when He did, we learned to our great surprise that *He* wanted to be "in relationship" with *us*. He came to earth to let us know that He was in love with His creation and had made it His great delight. The whole story of the Bible is the story of God's love reaching out to us — through the creation itself, through the journey to freedom from bondage, through roaring mountains and burning bushes and lightning writing on tablets of stone. Through the loving guidelines that would prevent our self-destruction, through the warnings of prophets, through a deep longing in the soul of us all — God wooed and reached.

Finally, God Himself came as one of us to touch us where we hurt, to heal us where we bled, to lift us when we fell, to fill a place so deep inside we didn't even recognize the hunger. From then on we knew not only that we *could* have a relationship with God but also that we *had* to have a relationship with Him. What would it take? What would He require?

Some said we had to dress certain ways. Others said we shouldn't have certain habits, shouldn't go certain places. Others thought there were styles of worship or expression that would make God show up. Some thought we had to be more pious, more thankful, more humble, more sacrificial, more disciplined.

But God said the requirement for relationship with Him is to want Him — to want Him more than anything else. Hunger is the requirement.

Thirst is what it takes. Pretty words, expensive gifts, burnt sacrifices, big buildings, fancy or plain clothes, status in the community, austerity in lifestyle — none of these move the heart of God. But hunger, need, a passion to truly know Him — these move the heart of God.

It moves the great heart of God when He sees us recognize our inadequacy, our immense neediness, our wayward hungers. Our vulnerability without arrogance or self-sufficiency brings Him closer to us than any sibling or parent or friend.

All other life-changes in us come as a natural result of hungering for Him, seeking His face, having an intimate relationship with Him. What a relief! What great news! We can't and don't need to remake ourselves to get God to notice us. He has already noticed. He longs for us to know Him. And when we come to know Him as He really is, this relationship changes us until we don't even recognize ourselves. We'll come — gradually and naturally — to look a lot like the object of our deepest affections!

Feelin' at Home in the Presence of Jesus

Feelin' at home in the presence of Jesus,
Hearing Him call me His own,
Just feelin' at home,
Feelin' at home.
Putting my feet right under His table,
Knowing I won't be alone,
Just feelin' at home,
Feelin' at home.

Feelin' at home in the presence of Jesus,
Needed and happy and free,
Just feelin' at home,
Feelin' at home.
Feelin' accepted and loved and forgiven,
A part of His warm family,
Just feelin' at home,
Feelin' at home.

> You couldn't have told me I'd find what I found:
> Contentment and peace from above;
> Feelin' at home in the presence of Jesus,
> Laying way back in His love.

> Warming myself by the fires of His Spirit,
> Camping right close to His throne,
> Just feelin' at home,
> Feelin' at home.

Feelin' at Home in the Presence of Jesus

───

I love the word *presence*. It implies that someone is physically where you are — in the room, in the house, at the table — here . . . now. It also says that person is not absent, not somewhere else.

When I was in elementary school, the teacher started each day by calling roll. When our names were read, we were to answer, "Present." Calling the roll wasn't just a benefit for the teacher and her records; it let us all know who would be there to choose for recess softball teams.

It told which whiz-kid spellers would be our spelling competition that day. It let us know whether there would be enough good roller skates to make the noon hour fun.

Over the years I have learned that having someone's body in the room or at the table doesn't necessarily mean that he or she is present. Many nights I have fixed a good dinner and called our family to the table. All the chairs are occupied and we bow our heads to pray, but it isn't long before someone says, "Earth to Dad! Earth to Dad!" or, "Suzanne, what's on *your* mind?" or, "Hey, Benj, wanna join us?"

This brings us to the other meaning of the word *presence:* an aura or a special chemistry that people have when they are present, or more specifically, their essence, their spirit. We've all known individuals about whom we've said, "She has a presence about her," or, "Just his presence makes me feel at ease."

Some presences have shaped my life. My father was a person whose presence felt like the Rock of Gibraltar. Even when a tornado hit our little village or an earthquake toppled the chimney of our farmhouse, I don't remember being afraid. Daddy was there and I knew he would know what to do. His presence meant security.

Mother, too, was a mighty presence in my life. Wise, insightful, creative, and wildly unpredictable, my mother filled our home with her presence. I knew when I ran into the house from school, from college, or from across the creek as a grown-up that I would find advice, surprise, beauty, reassurance, and comfort in my mother's presence.

I have known people in whose presence I never felt comfortable. My spirit could sense that under the surface of a quiet facade, a volcano just waited to erupt. Others' presences have made me feel sad for a brokenness deep inside and from long ago that I was helpless to reach or fix.

Some presences are intimidating. These are people who make me feel stupid or awkward, unsophisticated or ugly. Math majors in college always made me feel inept. I have met doctors whose office manner paralyzed into silence my questions about my own health and body.

I have learned, however, that truly great people are almost always easy to be around. Secure and knowledgeable, they have nothing to prove. When you leave their presence, you find yourself saying, "They were so down-to-earth." But in spite of being comfortable in the presence of a secure person of greatness, no one in their right mind would try to fake knowledge and wisdom in front of someone who is a real authority in some field. The best gift any of us can bring is honesty, not self-righteous pseudoconfidence. Knowing that you have nothing to bring but your real self tears down barriers and lets the authority simply enjoy you as a person.

Many stories in the Bible tell us that Jesus made regular people feel safe and at peace in His presence. Children climbed up on His lap; women didn't feel belittled or intimidated but felt encouraged to touch the hem of His garment, answer His questions about their personal lives, or invite Him to dinner. Fishermen and theologians were equally drawn to Him.

His friends loved being where He was and huddled around tables to discuss great issues with Him or escaped with Him in a boat to enjoy fellowship and good conversation. His students loved the practical way He taught them. The simple and uneducated felt valued by Him.

Yet Jesus made some people uncomfortable. Those with unwholesome agendas were agitated by His wisdom. Ulterior motives and phony spirituality were quickly exposed in His presence. Demonic dispositions were enraged by Him.

But what warmth there was for those left out in the cold by injustice. What joy for those who were sad! What comfort for the grief-stricken, and what acceptance and grace for those beaten and battered by the cruelties of life!

Long before Christ was born, Isaiah described the refreshing experience of those who would know the presence of Jesus:

The Spirit of the Sovereign LORD is on me, because the LORD has anointed me to preach good news to the poor. He has sent me to bind up the brokenhearted, to proclaim freedom for the captives and release from darkness for the prisoners, to proclaim the year of the LORD's favor and the day of vengeance of our God, to comfort all who mourn, and provide for those who grieve in Zion — to bestow on them a crown of beauty instead of ashes, the oil of gladness instead of mourning, and a garment of praise instead of a spirit of despair. They will be called oaks of righteousness, a planting of the LORD for the display of his splendor.

ISAIAH 61:1–3

I'll Worship Only at the Feet of Jesus

I went to visit the shrine of plenty
But found its storerooms all filled with dust.
I bowed at altars of gold and silver,
But as I knelt there, they turned to rust.

> So I'll worship only at the feet of Jesus;
> His cup alone: my Holy Grail.
> There are no other gods before Him.
> Just Jesus only will never fail.

The call of fortune made me a pilgrim
To journey to fame's promised heights.
But as I climbed, the promise faded,
And wind blew lonely through the night.

Just desert dust and empty shadow:
All promises that turn to lies.
The gods of earth fail and betray me.
You alone are my Truth and Life.

> So I'll worship only at the feet of Jesus;
> His cup alone: my Holy Grail.
> There are no other gods before Him.
> Just Jesus only will never fail.

I'll Worship Only at the Feet of Jesus

It is curious to most new millennium minds that the first and greatest commandment for both Judaism and Christianity is "Thou shalt have none other gods before me" (Deut. 5:7 KJV). Jesus echoed this commandment when He summed up all the law and the prophets and encapsulated His own mission statement by saying, "Thou shalt love the Lord thy God with all thy heart, and with all thy soul, and with all thy mind" and "love thy neighbor as thyself" (Matt. 22:37, 39 KJV).

The old word for what the commandments forbid is *idolatry*. Since we don't live in a multideity culture, we tend to think we aren't idolaters. Graven images, sun gods, moon goddesses, sacrifices to the Nile River, sacred cows: all these seem ridiculous to most religious American minds. "Of course we worship the one true God! Idolatry was in another time, in another place, right?"

In his book *Addiction and Grace*, Gerald May confronts our self-righteousness and calls it addiction, another word for idolatry.

> *"Nothing," God says, "must be more important to you than I am. I am the Ultimate Value, by whom the value of all other things must be measured and in whom true love for all things must be found. . . ."* It is addiction that keeps our love for God and neighbors incomplete. It is addiction that creates other gods for us. Because of our addictions, we will always be storing up treasure somewhere other than heaven, and these treasures will kidnap our hearts and souls and strength.[1]

We counter immediately, "I've never been addicted. I've never abused drugs. I'm not an alcoholic." Yet in truth, attachments to things and relationships other than God Himself usher us unwittingly into "addictions that make idolaters of us all."

---

[1]From *Addiction and Grace*. Written by Gerald G. May. Published by Harper and Row. © Copyright 1988 by Gerald R. May. All rights reserved. Used by permission.

Idolatry is the opposite of freedom. Jesus said, "If the Son sets you free, you will indeed be free" (John 8:36 LB). He is personified truth. And anything that tugs us from Him — even so-called good things — can beguile and addict us. Anything that becomes our pleasure center, taking the place of God as our measuring stick for joy, is addicting and idolatrous. Sadly, this loss of balance, this skewing of focus, is capable of eventually destroying the very pleasure it seems at first to deliver.

No wonder Jesus said, "Anyone who loves his father or mother [or son or daughter] more than me is not worthy of me" (Matt. 10:37). Such misplaced focus of our finest love will eventually latch itself on to its object and suck it dry, destroying it in the end. No husband, wife, child, or friend is able to fulfill our deepest needs. No lover can complete the picture, be our "missing piece." Only God is a source so infinite that our needs will not exhaust it. He is a source so boundless that out of it we can draw the love it takes to nurture all relationships and fill our deepest longings at the same time.

I have a habit of reading ads and listening to commercials. Ad agencies are pros at naming the deep spiritual needs we all share, then tying those needs to a promise of fulfillment through some product. What do we need? Acceptance? Happiness? Peace? A place to belong? Security? Love? To be valued? Things that promise to satisfy our longings are standing in line. Our economy runs on convincing us we can't live without products that didn't exist a decade ago, last year, last month!

Yet we drive the cars, furnish our houses with the couch and easy chair, cover our floors with the carpet or hardwood, send our kids to the schools, wear the designer lines and the makeup, carry the leather briefcases, and only grow more restless and empty.

Few of us would actually admit that we think products and artifacts could ever satisfy the hungers of the soul, yet Christians and non-Christians alike find it nearly impossible to resist the beguiling promises of an easy fix and then truly simplify our lives, refocus our affections, and embrace unadulterated truth without fear or hesitation.

Sadly, instead of keeping God the measuring stick for all joy and pleasure, we all too often let our addictions become the measuring stick for God. We attach our spiritual hungers to the things we invent to express our worship—our style, modes of expression, theological systems, "aids" to worship, certain emotional or cerebral or artistic experiences connected with religion.

Some of us have fallen for the high we get from doing good, helping others, for being applauded in one way or another. Our "god" might be building churches, holding meetings, influencing and motivating audiences, creating beautiful liturgy, evangelizing the neighborhood, feeding the poor. As good as these things are, they are not God Himself.

No wonder Jesus said to those who scoffed at Mary for "wasting" the precious perfume of her love at the feet of the Master, "She has done a beautiful thing to me. The poor you will always have with you" (Matt. 26:10b–11). He knew that helping the poor naturally results from adoring Him, but when helping the poor becomes the focus, it turns us into idolaters who have lost the joy of the journey with Him.

In the classic tales of King Arthur and his knights of the round table, Arthur searches for the Holy Grail — the cup that his Lord had offered to His friends that night in the Upper Room. It becomes a tangible reminder to Arthur and his knights to drink the cup of sacrifice and service, calling them to righteous living and noble deeds.

The search leads them into all kinds of adventures and conquests. In the process, the search for the grail becomes such an all-consuming quest that the dear Lord Himself fades from view.

As good as these men aspire to be, as urgent as their search becomes, they lose sight of the face of Jesus and His hands that held the cup.

The book of Hosea the prophet is a call to all who have ever gone off on adventures of misplaced affection. A dear yearning in the voice of God rings even through the warnings of destruction. Listen to the lover of our hearts: "I don't want your sacrifices — I want your love; I don't want your offerings — I want you to know me.... Oh Judah, for you also there is a plentiful harvest of punishment waiting — and I wanted so much to bless you!" (Hos. 6:6, 11 LB).

But what a merciful God we have! In spite of our unfaithful fickle hearts, His love calls us always back to the true center where we can find healing and wholeness. His resurrection has brought us the cup of joy.

> *Come, let us return to the Lord; it is he who has torn us — he will heal us. He has wounded — he will bind us up. In just a couple of days, or three at the most, he will set us on our feet again, to live in his kindness! Oh, that we might know the Lord! Let us press on to know him, and he will respond to us as surely as the coming of dawn or the rain of early spring.*
>
> *HOSEA 6:1–3 LB*

Thanks for Sunshine

Thanks for sunshine;
Thanks for love;
Thanks for flowers,
Rain from above.
Thanks for children,
For each girl and boy;
Thanks for laughter;
Thanks for their joy.

> *Lord, so many times I prayed so selfishly;*
> *Lord, so many times You blessed abundantly.*

Thanks for the promise
You'd make it all good.
For those who would trust You,
You said that You would.
So thanks for tomorrow;
Fill it with love;
We know that all good things
Come from above.

> *So this time, oh Lord, I don't want anything,*
> *I just want to say thanks for letting this old boy sing.*

> > *Thanks for labor;*
> > *Thanks for tears.*
> > *So this time, O Lord, I don't want anything.*
> > *I just want to say thanks for giving me a song to sing.*

Thanks for sunshine;
Thanks for love;
Thanks for flowers,
Rain from above.
So thank You,
Thank You, Lord.

Thanks for Sunshine

My sister and I have taken a tiny cottage just in sight of the ocean on an island for a week. It's a simple place surrounded by dunes and the native grasses, scrub oak, bayberry, and pine that are common here. Small yellow buttercups dot the grasses, and at night the crickets sing us to sleep.

Provisions are simple, reduced to bare essentials. It is all one would really ever need: a few plates, a skillet, a couple of cooking pans, a stove and refrigerator, and a washing machine. This morning I washed a load of laundry, which I hung out to dry on the clothesline strung between the posts holding up the second-floor deck.

As I clipped the clothespins to the towels, I could see my grandmother's hands going through the same washday ritual, and the fragrance of air-dried sheets wafted through my memory. This small task of doing the laundry is a strong cord tying me to all the generations of women in my gene pool, making me a part of the fabric we have together woven with the strong fibers of our days.

It seemed, as I gazed across the field of tall grasses, I could see a path that began here, seaside sandy, where I stand today. It seemed to wind its way across this moor to some distant place where it blended into a path of Indiana clay, then joined a trail of Michigan loam. A bit farther it became a country road of Missouri red dirt that led all the way to the emerald hillsides of Ireland and across the yellow rapefields of England and beyond to the practical farms of Germany.

I know there is a multigenerational presence in me that has melted into what I now know only as a day in this woman's life. And I know, too, that the ritual of this morning's tasks is not at all simple. I do what I do the way my mother taught me, and her mother taught her. I feel satisfaction in the task that someone made meaningful for me by the joyful doing of it before me: tidying a kitchen after breakfast, smoothing a freshly made bed, folding a clean white linen, sweeping a floor.

In a world searching for meaningful occupation, I'm thankful to those who taught me that meaning is in the soul of the doer and that all tasks are honorable when they are done with a grateful, joyous heart!

Jesus, You're the Center of My Joy

Jesus, You're the center of my joy;
All that's good and perfect comes from You.
You're the heart of my contentment,
Hope for all I do;
Jesus, You're the center of my joy.

When I've lost my direction,
You're the compass for my way;
You're the fire and light when nights are long and cold.
In sadness You're the laughter
That shadows all my fears;
When I'm all alone, Your hand is there to hold.

Jesus, You're the center of my joy;
All that's good and perfect comes from You.
You're the heart of my contentment,
Hope for all I do;
Jesus, You're the center of my joy.

You are why I find pleasure
In the simple things in life;
You're the music in the meadows and the streams.
The voices of the children,
My family and my home,
You're the source and finish of my highest dreams.

Jesus, You're the center of my joy;
All that's good and perfect comes from You.
You're the heart of my contentment,
Hope for all I do;
Jesus, You're the center of my joy.

Jesus, You're the Center of My Joy

ill and I have received many awards for our music and writing. We never cease to be amazed when a song that came out of the reality of our lives and everyday walk with God connects with fellow pilgrims who find hope and encouragement from it on the way. Awards seem somehow out of place for such a process, yet we are always grateful and honored when they come.

The one award in our trophy case that is to me among the most treasured is the Stellar Award, given for the Black Gospel song of the year, for the song "Jesus, You're the Center of My Joy," which we wrote with Richard Smallwood, a fine musician and songwriter. The award was presented at the famous Apollo Theatre in Harlem, where many African-American performers and artists have gotten their start. What a night it was to hear the Mississippi mass choir, Whitney Houston and her mother, Sissy, and dozens of other amazing communicators singing in this place, which seems to vibrate with the pain and glory of those who have ever sung there.

The song itself began for Bill one day in Nashville when he and Richard got together to write some music. For me it began when Bill handed me a tape and said, "Can you write lyrics to this melody?"

I listened to the music and found it haunting. It seemed to be saying, "Jesus, You're the center of my joy. All that's good and perfect comes from You." The rest of the chorus sort of dictated itself. "You're the heart of my contentment, hope for all I do. Jesus, You're the center of my joy."

I listened to their melody for the verse and thought of "all that's good and perfect" in our lives, the things worth dying — and living — to keep. They are the simple things, the gentle things, yet the things that seem to be threatened the most when we get our priorities out of order.

As I wrote and considered life as God had ordered it in His Word and by the teaching and example of Jesus, I had to conclude that, indeed, all that God puts in our lives is always whole, perfect, and good. It is what we do to distort God's gifts that brings pain, dissatisfaction, unrest, bitterness, and a hunger that gnaws at our souls.

Food, for instance — that life-sustaining gift — is good for us when we keep it as near as possible to the way it grows. We know that what we have done to food — synthetic fertilizers, pesticides, herbicides, processing — has made food a commercial success, but for our tampering, the human family is paying dearly in cancer, allergies, attention disorders, and hundreds of others problems we may identify. But whole grains, green spring grasses and leaves, organically grown vegetables and fruits, fish from unpolluted waters, and poultry free to roam — all these are healthful and satisfying. Water, plentiful and pure, from deep underground springs that have never been tainted by chemicals and toxins carelessly used and discarded is good and necessary for every function of our bodies.

Relationships that are honest, pure, enriching, and true are the greatest of all treasures we can know in this life. But our fallen nature gets in the way and destroys the very things we need and treasure so much. Only relationships redeemed by grace can dare to love, trust, forgive, accept, give the benefit of the doubt, go the second mile, and relinquish paralyzing control. Only the cross can pry loose the strangling grip of selfishness from the neck of our relationships and let the breath of God flow into the hidden interiors of our marriage, our home life, and our friendships.

Beauty comes from God. All that is beautiful and unspoiled in nature is the work of His hand. All that is created by the artist, the decorator, the architect, the musician, the writer, the landscaper, the craftsman — all that is aesthetically comforting to the soul — is schooled by the laws of the Creator who made light and shadow, mountains and plains, color and texture, sound and the instrument that can hear it. Even in an ugly, rude, polluted, and noisy world, beauty surprisingly breaks through to hearts and minds that long for it. And wherever there is harmony, wherever there is peace, wherever there is light and hope, there is God, striving with our spirits, drawing us like a magnet back to the center of His heart.

In this world, it is easy to lose our focus, break loose from our moorings, be sidetracked by the artificial trappings of our culture. But God always offers a way back to the center where joy lives. We can consult the manual; we can read the map for directions back home. We can follow these simple instructions (see Phil. 4:4–9 MESSAGE):

1. "Celebrate God all day, every day. I mean, revel in him!"
2. "Don't fret or worry. Instead of worrying, pray. . . . It's wonderful what happens when Christ displaces worry at the center of your life."

3. "You'll do best by filling your minds and meditating on things true, noble, reputable, authentic, compelling, gracious — the best, not the worst; the beautiful, not the ugly; things to praise, not things to curse."

4. The promised results are guaranteed, no matter the circumstances of our lives: God, "who makes everything work together, will work you into his most excellent harmonies."

There have been times when, even trying to do God's work, we have let other things take center stage in our lives. Often others would consider those things to be "ministry."

But *Jesus* must be our joy center. When He is, we get joy from everything that is good. When He is not the center of our joy, we get jaded; we become cynical even about God-things, and our joy in everything drains away.

Lord, save us from seeking anything except You. Check our spirits when we seek Your work, Your will, Your gifts, or Your attributes. Remind us constantly that when we have You — a deep, growing, abiding relationship with You — all things will be added to our lives without our even noticing. This day we do not ask You to bless what we are doing. We do ask that You reveal to us what You are doing and let us be a part of it. That, we know, will place us in the joy center of the universe. Amen.

Get All Excited

Get all excited, go tell ev'rybody that Jesus Christ is King!
Get all excited, go tell ev'rybody that Jesus Christ is King!
Get all excited, go tell ev'rybody that Jesus Christ is King;
Jesus Christ is still the King of kings, King of kings.

You talk about people,
You talk about things that really aren't important at all;
You talk about weather,
You talk about problems we have here at home and abroad;
But friend, I'm excited about a solution for the world —
I'm gonna shout and sing!
Jesus Christ is still the King of kings, King of kings!

Get All Excited

A football game inspired this song. Excitement mounted as the score was tied with only a few minutes left to play. Fans from both sides abandoned their seats, screaming and waving banners. The stands were a circus of color and motion; the decibels rose to an almost deafening level.

The atmosphere in the stadium hovered on that fine line between exciting hysteria and terrifying emotion. Just one fan losing control, one derogatory comment over the line, and pandemonium would have broken out.

Grown men jabbed the air with their fists as they chanted cheers for their team. Some fans jumped up and down, hugging anyone who wore their team's colors. Some slapped the person in front of them on the back every time a few inches were gained on the field.

Inhibitions that had kept people proper and even uncommunicative were thrown to the wind. Tomorrow everyone would be decorous again, but today for a few hours, the restrictions of expectations were gone. And this reckless abandon was over a game between two football teams on an autumn afternoon.

On the way home Bill and I talked about the game and the hysteria that had swept us up with the fans. "It's good to see people get that excited about something," Bill said. "Too bad so much energy has to be spent on a football game. If guys got that excited over the Lord, someone would think they'd lost their minds."

We pondered his words as we drove on. A skirmish between two teams on a football field is nothing compared with the battle between the forces of evil and the power of God. When we sinful human beings encounter the love and grace of a God who has "taken the hit" for us, we should really respond with excitement. Yet we sit sedately in church and sing about a life-changing confrontation as if we were having a polite parlor conversation.

The next morning was Saturday. I made coffee and started to feed the kids. Bill took his coffee into the family room and began to play with a new tune on the piano. The fun upbeat rhythm lured our little Suzanne into the room to listen to what he was playing. It wasn't long before he called me. I took the other two little ones with me to hear what Bill was singing.

Before long he and the rest of us were singing this catchy little song that has become the signature of our concerts over the years. It has been translated into several languages, but perhaps its rhythm is best in Spanish. No matter the language in which it is sung, the message is universal: we talk about and get excited about the things that really matter to us. If Jesus really matters to us, He will make His way into our conversations. We will talk about Him as naturally and as enthusiastically as a football fan talks about the greatest game of the season!

Overwhelming victory is ours through Christ who loved us enough to die for us. For I am convinced that nothing can ever separate us from his love.

ROMANS 8:37–38 LB

Part Two

❧ ✦ ☙

The song of Jesus was never meant to be a solo. Such joyful music wells up and soon spills over into every area of our lives. It sings its way into places that are not always safe, but a new set of values makes us fearless and at peace.

I Walked Today Where Jesus Walks

I walked today where Jesus walks,
Down the crowded streets
Where the children have no place to play,
Where the homeless wait
For life to take them in —
Yes, I walked with Jesus there today.

I saw the Lord behind the eyes
Of the broken men,
And I felt His wounded hand reach out.
As the careless traffic sped
Along the other side,
I saw Jesus walk the streets today.

Where the least of all
Find no place to turn,
And they fall without a name —

Jesus walks with these —
The hungry and the lost —
Off'ring water from the cup and bread —
The Bread of Life, the Living Stream,
Where teeming millions cross
To find that God, yes, God Himself, walks there.

I Walked Today Where Jesus Walks

In May of 1985 our daughter Suzanne and I took a university class together in urban ministries. The structure for the May term course was two weeks of class time in which we read and discussed several fiction and nonfiction books about harsh urban life, followed by two weeks of living and working in the reality of two urban centers, Washington, D.C., and New York City.

In these two cities, we stayed in the sparsest of accommodations — the Vanderbilt YMCA in downtown Manhattan and the basement of a

Presbyterian church in the center of Washington, where we slept dorm style on camp cots. Each day we were involved in inner-city ministries, feeding the hungry, rebuilding old burned-out buildings for urban housing, and visiting and serving in soup kitchens, missions of mercy, and shelters.

This experience was so life changing that I have never been nor will ever be able to see life — mine or anyone else's — in the same light. I have been changed by the realization that Jesus identified with the poor in body and the poor in spirit and that as His disciples we must also identify with the poor.

I came face to face with the words of Jesus, "Whenever you did one of these things to someone overlooked and ignored, that was me — you did it to me" (Matt. 25:40 MESSAGE), and have become poignantly aware that I must recognize His eyes peering at me through the eyes of "the least of these." I have been forced more and more out of the judgment business (the cardinal sin of playing God) and into the grace and mercy business (the only work given us to do).

At the end of that trip, I chronicled some of what I was beginning to learn about the Jesus I had followed into the city. What follows is something I wrote in an effort to sort out this urban experience. Later, the piece I wrote about it gave birth to the song lyric "I Walked Today Where Jesus Walks." Greg Nelson put it to music and Larnelle Harris, with the Gaither Vocal Band, was the first to record and perform the song. The passion for the city and its special cries of need has never left me. Even now, as I recall each vivid image, I am reminded what a special place is reserved in the heart of God for the city.

Bethlehem, Galilee, Gethsemane — He walked there. But today Christ walks the concrete sidewalks of Times Square, 47th Street, and Broadway. And as He walks, His feet are soiled — not with the sand of the seashore or the reddish dust of the Emmaus Road but with the soot and filth of the city.

He walks the Great White Way, and His face is lit by the gaudy neon signboards of materialism. He walks in the shadows of the dark alleyways, where faces are not lit at all.

He walks with children and goes where they are taken when they are enticed and bartered to gratify some sick perversion. He walks the steaming hallways of welfare hotels, where mothers cry themselves to sleep in worry and despair.

He does not sleep but lies beside the broken in their vermin-infested shelters and hears the homeless groan in their delirium; He walks between the bodies as they wake, touching heads of matted hair, offering a hand to lift the men and women who are stiff from lying on the drafty floor.

He walks the streets of Harlem and Chinatown, Brooklyn and the Bronx, and stops to stand with those whose buildings smolder, whose sons are lost to drugs, whose mothers are evicted, whose daughters sell their bodies for a meal.

He walks the subway aisles, offering His seat to the old, the weary, the pregnant. He is jostled with the throngs at rush hour and reads the signs that offer satisfaction from Jack Daniels or a hot line to call to rid one's body of a growing life.

He is pushed and shoved through Grand Central Station, elbowed and ignored, yet in the crowd He feels a measure of virtue flow from His being and searches the faces for an honest seeker passing by.

Christ walks the city. I've seen Him there. I've seen His blistered, broken feet, galled by wearing shoes without socks. He walks the city on children's feet that grow too fast to stay in shoes at all. He walks the street in high-heeled shoes that pinch the toes but attract the client.

He walks the city. He stands behind a table serving breakfast, drives a truck that carries sandwiches to the grates where homeless sleep to garrison themselves against the cold. He climbs the narrow staircases of burned-out buildings and restores them into homes again. He paints and disinfects and hauls out trash.

I've seen Christ stand by a dental chair, fixing worn-out teeth. I've seen Him tutoring a dropout and heard Him say, "Keep reaching for the sky." Christ holds a baby whose mother is a child herself — so needing to be mothered — and holds that mother's mother in His arms at night when prayers become such groanings that they cannot be uttered. He groans with them all — a mother to three generations of the motherless.

Christ walks the city and carves saints in stone for some cathedral — the cherubim and seraphim with faces of the street. He weaves the fibers from tattered rags into a lovely tapestry. Christ dances when He Himself can find no other way to say "I love you" to a world in which there is left no word for Love. He acts out the story of how that Love invaded humankind, for the only Story tells the story. Christ incarnate. Christ the living, walking parable takes to the stage of the streets to be the Story.

Christ the Advocate walks the city. "You have an advocate with the Father," He said. That is done. But now the powerless need an advocate with the government — to help with the red tape, the powers that be. Christ walks there. Jesus, "our lawyer in heaven," walks the city to become a lawyer in the streets — filling out welfare forms, phoning caseworkers, petitioning agencies, drafting legislation to protect the poor. Christ the Advocate walks the city.

Christ walks the city's Ivy Halls, where students debate His existence. He holds out His nail-scarred hands to the agnostics and invites them to touch and see. He is there at the gay caucus and the feminist rally and the meeting for the apartheid demonstration. He who is question and answer, He who sets brother against brother yet whispers "peace, be still" to the turbulent waves, walks here.

Christ walks the halls of government, and in His presence statesmen hammer out the laws. The just and the unjust, the honest and the ruthless, those who struggle for truth and those who live the lie convene in His presence, for Christ walks the marble halls of government, sifting the wheat from the chaff.

Christ walks the corridors of justice. He is in night court and stands with the accused and the accuser. He who is truth and mercy and justice weighs them both and walks both to the judge's chamber and the prisoner's cell.

Christ is no stranger to locks and bars. He paces with the convicted in their narrow space and hears the curses of despair. Yes,

Christ is present in the prisons, where fear has built walls around the heart thicker than the walls that guard against escape and higher than the barbed wire that makes an ugly frame for the gray skies. He walks the empty corridors and offers the key of freedom to whomever would become citizens of a new country, a different kingdom. It is the very key He offers to the judge, who is also a captive, a key that makes both the sentencer and the condemned free men and women — family.

Christ calls all to Communion. The table of the Eucharist is spread. He takes the bread. He is the Bread. He breaks it, breaks Himself, and offers this brokenness to us, explaining that if we take it, we ourselves must be broken and consumed. He takes the cup. It is the pouring out of Himself. He says, "Won't you, too, be poured out with me?"

The table is long and spans centuries. Some leave the table to go in search of silver. Some chairs were empty from the start, for though many were invited, some had wives to marry, parents to bury, houses to build, empires to manage.

Those who have come are a motley blend of ages and nationalities, races and genders. But they are all poor and hungry and needy. Slowly, they break the bread — again and again — and lift their morsels to their mouths. It does not go down easily. Sometimes it sticks in the throat . . . until the wine is passed. The pressed and poured-out fruit washes away the dryness.

The bread — "My flesh" — and the wine — "My life's blood" — together make a sacrament of joy, and the rite becomes a celebration of paradox. In the breaking, we have become whole. In the pouring out, we have been filled. In bringing our poverty and hunger and need, we have been made rich. In daring to sit with seekers whose differences we did not understand, we have been made one.

Christ the paradox walks the city. He is the broken, and He is the healer. He is the hungry, and He is the Bread of Life. He is the homeless, yet it is He who says, "Come to Me all you who are overloaded, and I will be your resting place." He is the loser who makes losing the only way to win. He is the omnipotent who calls all who follow to choose powerlessness and teaches us how by laying down all power in heaven and on earth. He is the sick, and He is the wholeness. He who said, "I thirst," is Himself the Living Water who promises we will never thirst again.

Just as the disciples in the Emmaus house recognized their Lord through the broken bread and the shared cup, so our blindness turns to sight in Holy Communion, and we see Him for who He truly is.

To Get This Close

I didn't know I had to come this far to get this close;
I'm learning that You're nearest when Your children need You most.
Without You I have nothing that I could ever boast,
But it's worth it all to come this far, so I could get this close.

The road You chose for me to walk at times was rough and steep.
The winds would howl through caverns carved between the boulders deep.
And there were nights when lumps of fear would rise up in my throat,
So when I tried to sing Your song, I'd choke on every note.

But now I see those were the times You guided me along
The narrow passes, and when I was weak, Your hand was strong.
And like a shepherd with his staff protects his wayward flock,
You crowded me into the clefted shelter of the rock.

The chilling night is gone, now, and the howling wind is still.
The morning sun is breaking just beyond the distant hill.
The shadows that I feared — I see now in light of day —
Were cast by peaks of alabaster all along the way!

I didn't know I had to come so far to get so close;
I'm learning, Lord, You're nearest when Your children need You most.
Without You I'd be nothing that I could ever boast,
But I'm so glad we've come this far, so we could be this close!

To Get This Close
and
Lord, Send Your Angels

❧

Bill's brother, Danny, had just had his second stem cell transplant in his fight against lymphoma, this time for an extended stay away from home at the University of Nebraska Medical Center in Omaha. It had been a strange Thanksgiving without him and his wife, Vonnie. He had been on all our minds as we shared our family ritual of placing our grains of Indiana corn in the little basket as it was passed around our country kitchen and each of us expressed what he or she was most thankful for since last we celebrated this festival of gratitude.

After Thanksgiving, Bill and I flew out to spend a couple of days with Danny and Vonnie in the hotel near the lymphoma clinic. When the hours were good, Danny talked and laughed; he and Bill told stories and recalled memories. Sometimes we made plans for Christmas, when they would be home. Vonnie had put a small Christmas tree in their hotel room and strung it with lights. She'd brought a tape player for music and had worked hard to make a home of that tiny space for the weeks of treatment and recovery.

Mostly, we all tried to think on the good things, to keep the atmosphere positive and cheerful, to encourage healing of the body and spirit every way we could. We prayed together and thanked God for leading us to Dr. Armitage and his team and for each nurse and physician who had a hand in the treatment process. We focused on how precious each moment was.

One afternoon while Danny was resting, Vonnie, Bill, and I had a chance to talk. "How are *you* doing?" I asked her. "Is there anything you need?"

"You know," she answered, "this has been very hard, but in a lot of ways it's been one of the richest times in our lives, too. So much good has come from it. Danny and I have had time to really love each other. God has taught us so much."

She stopped for a moment to consider. "It's just that I didn't know we'd have to come so far to get this close."

Her words were like a hot branding iron on my heart. That's it, of course! All things of eternal consequence are a process. The outcome, the purpose of God's process in us, always is the enrichment of our relationships with Him and with each other. It's all about relationship. I knew right away that her words would become a song. They were practically singing themselves into our hearts when she said them.

Hardly ever are things what they appear to be on the surface. The images that seem so threatening in the dark turn out to be totally different in the light of day. And the places into which we are shoved by the random happenings of life turn out to be the places nearest God's own heart; we emerge to realize we have been crowded into His sweet embrace.

Later, when Danny was home, he described an experience he had during his lowest moment. He had felt his life slipping away like sand between his fingers, and he seemed powerless to stop it. He remembered thinking, *I'm not going to make it. These toxins are going to kill me this time before they kill the cancer. I am dying.*

Then he said he opened his eyes to see his bed surrounded by little laughing children. Some were peeking over the foot of the bed; some were beside him, some at his head. He could see their little curls bobbing as they sang happy tunes as children do; they grinned at him.

A simple rhyme his mother used to recite to him and Bill when they were little came back to him.

Five little angels around my bed
One at the foot, one at the head,
One to watch, and one to pray
And one to take my fears away.

"Immediately," he said, "I knew they were angels, and I knew I would live. The spirit of fear left me, and I slept like a child."

Several months later that experience, too, became a song. I was gone to a speaking engagement and Bill was home alone. He had had a difficult week, and that night, especially, problems seemed to loom bigger than life. He couldn't sleep, so he got up and opened the Bible to Psalm 91.

He will give his angels charge over thee, to keep thee in all thy ways.
They shall bear thee up in their hands. . . . Because he hath set his love upon
me, therefore will I deliver him: I will set him on high, because he hath
known my name. He shall call upon me, and I will answer him: I will be
with him in trouble: I will deliver him, and honor him. With long life will
I satisfy him, and show him my salvation.

VERSES *11–12, 14–16* ASV

Bill went to the piano and began to write a chorus.

Lord, send Your angels to watch over me;
I'm so afraid of the dark.
Lord, send Your angels to watch over me.
Wrap me in sheltering arms.

As soon as morning came, he called our daughter Suzanne. "Could you come over and listen to this song I've started?" he asked her. As soon as she could get away, Suzanne came to the house. These are her words:

When I arrived at the house, Dad asked me if I had ever really read the ninety-first Psalm. I sat at the kitchen counter and absorbed that comforting passage about how God covers us "with his feathers, and under his wings" we find refuge. The eleventh verse says, "For he will command his angels concerning you to guard you in all your ways; they will lift you up in their hands, so that you will not strike your foot against a stone" (NIV). Dad told me that he had been awake in the middle of the night, worried about the concerns of the day, and that he had opened his Bible to that beautiful Scripture. "You know," he said, "most people I know, men in particular, don't have much trouble fighting against enemies they can see. It's the enemies they cannot see, the powers and principalities of darkness, that plague them with fear."

I thought, *Sometimes we all need to be reminded that even in the "unseen" battles that rage around us every day, we have an advocate in God the Father, and He always sends His angels when the "night is closing in."*

Dad had a melody he had written in the night. He went to the piano and played it for me to see if I could write some verses for his chorus. The melody was so sweet and simple I knew I needed to keep the words pure and simple too — childlike even. I wrote him two verses, and together we sang them to his music.

The impact of the song was immediate. Three of the young women who travel with the Homecoming Friends sang it that very weekend. The audience's response let us know that fears in the night are a common, human experience. But the promise of God is that perfect love casts out all fear. The only perfect love is the love of our heavenly Father, who promises to send His angels to watch over us, to bear us up, and to keep us in all our ways.

Rest well.

Lord, Send Your Angels

When I'm alone and the light slowly fades —
Cold, with the night closing in —
I know the shadow of Almighty wings;
Lord, won't You send them again?

> Lord, send Your angels
> To watch over me;
> I'm so afraid of the dark.
> Lord, send Your angels
> To watch over me.
> Wrap me in sheltering arms.

> Shield me,
> Keep me,
> Hold me in Your arms.

Sometimes the child inside of me cries
With fears of the dangers unseen
And questions with answers I can't seem to find;

> Then You send Your angels to me.

Let Freedom Ring

Deep within, the heart has always known that there is freedom
Somehow breathed into the very soul of life.
The prisoner, the powerless, the slave have always known it;
There's just something that keeps reaching for the sky.

Even life begins because a baby fights for freedom,
And songs we love to sing have freedom's theme;
Some have walked through fire and flood to find a place of freedom,
And some faced hell itself for freedom's dream.

> Let freedom ring wherever minds know what it means to be in chains.
> Let freedom ring wherever hearts know pain.
> Let freedom echo through the lonely streets where prisons have no key —
> We can be free and we can sing,
> "Let freedom ring!"

God built freedom into every fiber of creation,
And He meant for us to all be free and whole;
But when my Lord brought freedom with the blood of His redemption,
His cross stamped "pardoned" on my very soul!

I'll sing it out with every breath and let the whole world hear it —
This hallelujah anthem of the free!
Iron bars and heavy chains can never hold us captive;
The Son has made us free and free indeed!

> Let freedom ring down through the ages from a hill called Calvary!
> Let freedom ring wherever hearts know pain.
> Let freedom echo through the lonely streets where prisons have no key —
> We can be free and we can sing:
> "Let freedom ring!"

Let Freedom Ring

One morning on the national news, there was a story about a young African-American police officer whose associates at the department met him one morning on duty dressed in the hooded garb of the Ku Klux Klan. Even women on the office staff and other department employees joined to taunt and frighten him. The prank went on a long time before they told him it was a joke and had him pose for pictures with them all in their costumes of discrimination.

On the news, this handsome young father was being interviewed by a reporter about the incident.

"How did you react?" the reporter asked.

"I was terrified on the inside, but all I could think to do was smile," he answered. "When I got home, I sobbed like a child."

Later the offenders, fearing reprisals and wanting to take back the photos they gave him, threatened the officer.

As I watched this young man trying to process such a deep and ugly violation by those he thought he knew, by those who served with him day by day under an oath to uphold justice, I felt powerful emotions rise within me. I felt anger at the indignity and at the violation of so many of the codes that hold any decent society together. I felt deep sadness at the breaking of the human spirit and the robbery of the self-respect of a fellow human being. I felt brokenness in my soul as I saw his pain and realized that all of us are capable of hurting each other deeply.

I left my house to go to the village for breakfast. As I sipped hot coffee, I watched a toddler across the room struggle to escape his mother's arms. He wanted to explore the café and then, perhaps, get close enough to slip through the screen door into the morning sunshine.

Every person innately longs to be free. This toddler knew it even in the womb. The time clock kicked in one day and the same little body that had been content to grow in the security of that liquid environment began to make its way — force its way — through the narrow confines of the birth canal to a place where it could be free. The passion to be free is built into the very fiber of creation: the seedling pushing against and bursting from the protective casing that carried it to its resting place; the gazelle racing from a predator; the squirrel, high above the ground, leaping to a distant limb to escape the competition.

Since the fall of mankind, people have used others to achieve their objectives. From the building of the kingdoms of Egypt and Rome to the present conflict between the Serbs and the ethnic Albanians in Kosovo, the strong have taken advantage of the weak. But the dream of freedom cannot be snuffed out by force or manipulation. Sooner or later, people will have their freedom — sometimes at any cost.

"What happens to a dream deferred?" asked the poet Langston Hughes.

> *Does it dry up*
> *Like a raisin in the sun?*
> *Or fester like a sore —*
> *And then run?*
> *Does it stink like rotten meat?*
> *Or crust and sugar out —*
> *Like syrupy sweet?*
> *Maybe it just sags*
> *Like a heavy load.*
> *Or does it explode?*[1]

---

[1]"Dream Deferred." Written by Langston Hughes. Alfred A. Knopf, publishers. © Copyright 1951 Langston Hughes from *Selected Poems of Langston Hughes*. All rights reserved. Used by permission.

In our times, perhaps the greatest example of the irrepressible passion for freedom is the people's reaction after the post–World War II communist takeover of what became known as East Germany.

Because so much land was taken out of private hands and forced into collective control and because of the repression of private trade in the German Democratic Republic (as East Germany was called in 1958), thousands of refugees fled to the West. In 1959, 144,000 fled. The number of refugees rose to 199,000 in 1960 as conditions worsened. In the first seven months of 1961, 207,000 left, including a huge number of the nation's brightest minds — doctors, dentists, engineers, and teachers. It is estimated that by 1961, 2.7 million people had left since the German Democratic Republic was established in 1949.

On August 13, 1961 — a Sunday morning — under the communist leadership of Erich Honecker, the GDR began to block off East Berlin with paving stones, barricades, and barbed wire. Railway and subway services to West Berlin were halted, cutting off the 60,000 or so commuters who worked in West Berlin. A few days later, the GDR began building a wall.

One year after the first barricades went up, an eighteen-year-old man named Peter Fechter was the first of more than a hundred to be shot and killed while trying to escape. But as the wall grew higher, as more and more guards kept watch, as the death area behind the wall widened, as the trench to stop vehicles deepened, the number of escape attempts only increased.

In Berlin, the wall stretched sixty-six miles, but people escaped by tunneling under it or by leaping over it from the windows of houses nearby into nets or onto the pavement. Soon the government ordered that the houses be evacuated and the windows bricked shut. Eventually, the buildings were demolished. Patrol trucks, watchdogs, watchtowers, bunkers, and trenches were added to the border area. Then, behind the wall, a second wall was constructed.

Yet people continued to escape.

In one of the more dramatic escapes, two families secretly bought small amounts of nylon cloth — eventually enough to sew a hot air balloon. They waited until midnight and then drove to a deserted field and launched their craft. Twenty-three minutes it remained aloft before the burner died, long enough to carry four adults and four children to their freedom. Back in East Germany, the sale of nylon was restricted and there was a ban on the sale of rope and twine.

No one knows exactly how many people escaped in the twenty-eight years the Berlin Wall stood. The wall became a symbol of all obstructions to freedom. Instead of stopping the free flow of people and ideas, it provided a tangible object that epitomized the barriers which the human spirit felt challenged to conquer.

It was a sentence from President Kennedy's speech during his visit to Berlin in June of 1962 that lent words to the struggle for freedom. Throwing out the speech given him by speechwriters, Kennedy wrote a new one while riding through the streets of West Berlin, where between one and two million Germans roared and cheered for four hours. At checkpoint Charlie, he climbed alone up to the viewing stand. Suddenly, in a far-off window of an East Berlin apartment, three women appeared waving handkerchiefs — a dangerous and risky gesture. Kennedy, realizing their risk, stood in silence facing the women in tribute to them. Then he squared his shoulders and began the speech that let the world know how universal is the spirit of freedom. He concluded the speech with the historic words, "Ich bin ein Berliner. I am a Berliner!"

We all are Berliners at heart because we all long to be free. The world knew in its gut that the wall would never work. It stood from 1961 until 1989, yet Kennedy's empathetic sentence and that simple gesture from those women in the gray East Berlin window predicted that it would crumble.

Down through history, dictators and philosophies have attempted to enslave the human spirit. Blood has flowed like rivers in the fight to regain human dignity. The Magna Carta, the Bill of Rights, the Declaration of

Independence, and the Emancipation Proclamation have taken their places with other great instruments of liberation to testify to the human passion for freedom. The official seals of governments were burned onto these documents that have deeply affected our own way of life.

But never has a document of freedom had the power to alter the course of history and change human lives like the declaration bearing the bloodstained brand of the cross. And this seal is burned not on a piece of paper but on the very souls of all who were enslaved by sin. The document is a simple invitation: "Come unto me, all ye that labor and are heavy laden, and I will give you rest" (Matt. 11:28 KJV).

Prison bars, heavy chains, dungeons, concentration camps, and shackles: none of these can hold a candle to the bondage of the human soul devised by the father of lies. But no release, no emancipation, no pardon can bring freedom like that bought at Calvary. That is freedom indeed! Let freedom ring!

Oh, the Precious Blood of Jesus

Fathomless the depths of mercy —
Endless flow the tides of grace —
Shore to shore His arms of welcome —
Sky to sky His warm embrace.

> Oh, the precious blood of Jesus!
> Oh, the sea of His great love!
> This shall be my song forever —
> Earth is mine, and heav'n above!

As no stone escapes the tempest,
There's no sin love's waves can't find
Hiding in the buried crevice,
Deep within the human mind.

His dear blood so free and costly,
Restless, rolling like the sea,
Washes over my dark spirit,
Cleansing and transforming me.

> Oh, the precious blood of Jesus!
> Oh, the sea of His great love!
> This shall be my song forever —
> Earth is mine, and heav'n above!

Oh, the Precious Blood of Jesus

~

I'm not sure when I first heard the story on the news about the grisly pickax murder of two people in Texas by a drug-crazed twenty-four-year-old woman and her boyfriend. The woman and her boyfriend had broken into the couple's apartment to steal motorcycle parts but were surprised by the couple and killed them. By the time I really began to pay attention to the story, the man had died in jail of a liver disease and the woman had been on death row for several years.

I do remember channel surfing one night and coming across an interview with this young woman. She was a pretty girl with dark hair and a calm face, and she was answering questions about her crime and her life circumstances that led to it. She seemed to be answering honestly without excuse as she described the mental state she had been in at the time and the horrible details of the murder.

Then she began to tell the interviewer that her life had been completely changed by an encounter with Jesus in jail. At first, I thought, *Oh, yeah. Another jailhouse conversion.* But the longer I listened, the more convinced I became that this person who had known nothing at all about God had experienced a genuine life-changing encounter with Jesus. She talked about her crime as if it had been in another life, committed by another person — a person she vividly remembered but could no longer claim to be.

The interviewer said, "You made an unusual request for a prisoner on death row. You asked for a dictionary. Could you explain why you wanted a dictionary?"

The young woman then began to tell about her childhood, about dropping out of school early and becoming a prostitute and a drug user like her mother had been. She had never developed much of a vocabulary or learned good communication skills. But now that God had changed her heart and filled her with such an overwhelming love for people, she wanted to be able to have the right words to tell what He had done for her, should the opportunity arise.

I called Bill in to hear this. There was a quiet urgency in her voice, yet a peace in her expression. "I think she is telling the truth," I told Bill. "This is a real conversion if I've ever seen one."

In the months that followed, there were from time to time commentators who speculated that Karla Faye Tucker was just another death row con artist trying to get a reprieve. Some said she had nothing to gain by this conversion story, that it would be more likely to work against her.

But a comment by a New York reporter who had followed Karla Faye Tucker over the whole fourteen years of her imprisonment was the most intriguing. The reporter concluded that she didn't know whether she believed in this Jesus or not; she'd never been a religious person. But after following this story from the beginning, she said, "I am convinced that Karla believes in Him." She was in the process of writing a book about the case.

Later that winter Larry King also interviewed Karla Faye. He opened the interview by saying, "Our guest for the full hour is a lady you have probably come to know or have read about. She is Karla Faye Tucker, and she is scheduled to be executed February 3, by lethal injection in this prison."

The camera zeroed in on King and his guest.

King continued, "Does it get worse every day?"

"No. It gets a little more exciting every day."

"Interesting choice of words, Karla."

"Yes."

"Exciting how?"

"Just to see how God is unfolding everything . . . and it's a blessing to be a part of it, and it's exciting to know God has a plan for this."

They went on to discuss her case, the possibility of pardon by Governor Bush, and the whole story of her life. Her chances of getting a last-minute reprieve were remote. Bush had never pardoned anyone on death row in Texas. But she was amazing as she kept bringing the discussion of all the issues swirling around this case back to the wonder of God's grace.

If her case was not commuted, King finally asked her after nearly an hour of questioning, would she doubt her faith?

"No, I would not," she answered.

"You would go into that room — I guess it's a room, huh?"

"Yes."

"Bravely?"

"I would," Karla answered. "I would go in there still speaking out for the love of God. I mean, if He doesn't . . . if He allows this to happen, that's okay. He's already saved my life. My life's already been saved. And He gave me a second chance. I didn't deserve it . . . by His mercy I was given that, so whatever He wants to do with my life now, I'll walk that with Him, whatever He chooses. I am just thankful that I got a chance."

The first weekend in February, we were to sing at a two-day Texas Homecoming event at the Fort Worth Convention Center. I had lost track of the Tucker case and hadn't thought much about it, until the day of the first evening concert. As we went to eat before the performance, we passed a newsstand. A headline read, "Texas Executes Karla Faye Tucker for Pickax Murder." I stopped to read the first line.

"Huntsville (AP) — Karla Faye Tucker, the born-again Christian who stirred debate over redemption on death row, was executed Tuesday for a 1983 pickax slaying in Houston. Tucker, the first woman executed in Texas since the Civil War, was pronounced dead at 6:45 P.M. EST, eight minutes after receiving a lethal injection."

The next night, the Homecoming Friends gave the concert as usual. Various artists sang until intermission, and then all the Homecoming Friends came out together for the second half to sit on the stage and sing as a group.

I'm not sure how to explain this; I've never had anything like it happen to me before or since. Bill always asks the audience to sing along with the group, but that night when all the singers and the audience sang together, I felt a presence with us, and my impression was that it was this woman I'd never met — Karla Faye Tucker — and that she was laughing, laughing like a child laughs when she runs down a hillside and jumps in a pile of leaves or springs off a diving board into a swimming pool.

At first I dismissed the impression, but as the concert went on, three times when the group and audience sang together, I felt this woman singing and laughing with childlike joy.

How can this be? I questioned myself. *What could this mean?* As if God gave me an answer, I realized that at last she was able to sing with the family of God, and if the family was gathered in Jesus' name, she could be with us. Whether we are on this side of eternity or the other, when the family gathers in Jesus' name, we are all together; we are all present in Him.

The next day we all flew to Hawaii to tape the *Hawaiian Homecoming* video. The shoreline of the place where we stayed was covered with huge black boulders that went from the water's edge to the green lawn that swept down from the hotel. A walk meandered along the ledge above the rocks. Because we were on the western side of the island, the lawn offered a perfect vantage point for enjoying the spectacular sunsets.

One evening I took my journal and a lawn chair down to the edge of the grass by the jagged shore to watch the sunset and write the day's happenings. During the course of the day, joggers and hotel guests had thrown things into the rocks: straws from their drinks, paper napkins, broken toys, discarded film packaging. By the end of the day, the rocks were littered with debris. But that week there had been a typhoon off Japan, and although the weather was beautiful in Hawaii, in the evening when the tides came in, the waves would crash against the shoreline with such force that the spray splashed twenty or more feet into the air, creating a sparkling lace of crystal against the scarlet sunset. The tremendous power of those waves loosened all the debris caught in the rocks — even things wedged deep in the crevices — leaving the boulders clean.

As I watched the tide clean this hidden garbage, I thought of Karla and the ocean of God's grace. "Is there a limit?" I had pondered many times since I first heard her story. Is there a limit to grace? Could God make an innocent child out of a pickax murderer? The wide ocean before me and the crashing tide in the scarlet sunset seemed to answer my question with certainty and power.

I interrupted my journal entry and began writing on the facing page. Words fell onto the paper as quickly as I could write them.

As no stone escapes the tempest,
There's no sin love's waves can't find
Hiding in the buried crevice,
Deep within the human mind.

His dear blood so free and costly,
Restless, rolling like the sea,
Washes over my dark spirit
Cleansing and transforming me.

It was a liberating answer: there is enough grace. For Karla. For me.

Dream On

When Joseph was a little boy, he was driven by his dreams.
God spoke to him, told him that He'd chosen him.
When others didn't understand, Joseph still believed,
And trusted Him, trusted and was willing to . . .

Dream on,
When the world just doesn't believe;
God has promised never to leave you all alone.
Dream on,
Follow hope wherever it leads;
In the seed of dreams there's promise of the dawn.
Dare to listen for the music,
Keep on following the star,
Morning can't be far,
Dream on.

There's not a valley deep enough that He can't lead you through.
He'll walk with you, walk the roughest roads with you.
No mountain ever rose so high that you can't climb with Him
And stand up tall, stand and look down on it all.

Dream on,
When the world just doesn't believe;
God has promised never to leave you all alone.
Dream on,
Follow hope wherever it leads;
In the seed of dreams there's promise of the dawn.
Dare to listen for the music,
Keep on following the star,
Morning can't be far,
Dream on.

Dream On

woke up this morning humming "Whispering Hope." Where the quaint, old song came from in the storage bin of my memory is anybody's guess, but there it was, working its way to the surface of my consciousness as I opened my eyes.

It surprised me. I had gone to sleep somewhat discouraged with myself and by the expectations of others — not exactly fertile ground for hope. Besides, the old song itself had always seemed rather bland and shallow to me as a maturing young quester. Not enough edge to it, I thought; not enough content.

So I spent today revisiting those old lyrics and repenting for the hasty judgment of my youth and my lack of attention to what I now realize is a profound and life-sustaining truth.

Soft as the voice of an angel —
Whispers a lesson unheard.
Hope — with a gentle persuasion
Whispers her comforting word:
"Wait! till the darkness is over;
Wait, till the tempest is passed.
Hope for the sunrise tomorrow,
After the shower is passed."
Whispering hope. Oh, how welcome thy voice!
Making my heart, in its sorrow, rejoice.

A few months ago my friend Peggy lost her thirty-four-year-old son — a tall, handsome, funny, strong, outdoorsy young man who was about to "turn out." No one quite knows what happened, but what began as a hiking expedition into one of his favorite places in the hills of Tennessee turned into a nightmare. A forest ranger appeared on Peggy's front porch with the news that Tom's body had been found at the foot of a wet slippery cliff.

Bill and I, too, have a strong, funny, grown son who is as dear to me as Tom is to Peggy. I tried to imagine how Peggy would ever climb through the despair of such an unfathomable loss. I'm not sure I could.

All the kind words, sympathetic letters, arms around the shoulders, assurances of continued prayer, admonitions to trust it all to the God who made us — all the good advice in the world — would not make it possible to crawl out of bed another morning and face another day full of other people's children and other families' joy.

Yet over these years since I first heard the song I woke up humming this morning, I have seen the amazing power of "the hope that is within us." I see it now in Peggy. And I am coming to know that some of the most quiet, unassuming truths are the most life changing and the most healing.

I am learning that hope cannot be conjured up by our will and grit. No, hope, like faith and love and patience and forgiveness, is a gift from God. As trite as this may sound, hope is more likely to wake us in the morning with the sound of whispering in our ear, "Come with Me; you can go on!" Hope is a vision, a dream, an inspiration projected on the screen of the soul from somewhere else.

Joseph was a receiver of hope. Even though he was in the pits at the hands of his wicked brothers, hope gave him the dream of a transformed family who would one day love each other. Even when he seemed to be rotting and forgotten in prison, the dream film flickered on.

As a childless old man, Abraham was a receiver of hope so insistent that he spent his evenings building a baby crib and a high chair.

David was a receiver of hope. He saw projected against a night sky the dream that lifted him from the sheepfold and finally placed him in the palace of the king.

Mary was visited by hope, a hope so certain that she endured through the bitter reality of a bloody cross to an empty tomb and, finally, to a hilltop in Bethany, where she watched her Hope — and the Hope of the world — return to the God who gave Him.

Paul's encounter with hope was anything but subtle. It did not whisper in the night. No, his vision blasted into his swaggering misdirected self-righteousness with such a force that it left him blinded by its reality and struck dumb before its awesome revelation.

Hope — the fragile, gentle, whispering, tough, enduring, awesome stuff dreams are made of — is the gift of God to every fainting heart.

Return to your fortress, O prisoners of hope.

ZECHARIAH 9:12

My Father's Angels

They're all above me, beneath me, before me —
They're all around me;
My Father's angels all protect me everywhere.

I could never stray so far
My Father would lose track of where I am:
Angels walk beside me,
Holding tightly to my hand.

They're all above me, beneath me, before me —
They're all around me;
My Father's angels all protect me everywhere.

Even when the night's so dark
I just can't see a thing in front of me,
I won't need to worry;
They can see; they see me.

They're all above me, beneath me, before me —
They're all around me;
My Father's angels all protect me everywhere.

My Father's Angels

~

*J*ust now there is an epidemic of what could be called angel mania. In an age of spiritual hunger, there are always commercial vendors of a pseudospirituality that demands nothing and is easily accessible. Hybrids of world religions, superstitions, magic tricks, and euphemistic rhetoric are peddled as prescriptions for the aching heart and fast food for the hungry soul.

In today's climate of spiritual newspeak, stories abound of angel sightings. Angel jewelry, angel T-shirts, and angel decor are purchasable icons for a religion in which there is no cross, no narrow road, and no judgment.

Fluffy ethereal images suggest a spiritual sensitivity that is in vogue, a religious club where admission is gained by using a few popular passwords like "the God within," "self-realization," "visualization," and "getting in touch with your inner reality."

But according to God's Word, real angels are servants of God who keep us focused on Christ Himself. They are not fluffy icons of a nebulous spirituality but powerful, mighty, and sometimes fearsome messengers and ministers to keep us from losing our way to the Way, the Truth, and the Life — Jesus.

Throughout Scripture are appearances of angels who do the bidding of God to minister to human beings. Here are just a few:

An angel of the Lord found and appeared to Hagar after her mistress, Sarai, mistreated her and caused her to run away from the household of Abraham. The angel named the child in her womb Ishmael, promised her many descendants, and sent her back home to Sarai to have her child.

The angel of the Lord shouted at Abraham from heaven as he drew back his knife to kill his son, Isaac, in obedience to God. "Do not lay a hand on the boy," the angel said. "Do not do anything to him. Now I know you fear God, because you have not withheld from Him your son, your only son." There caught in a tangled thicket was a lamb to be offered as a sacrifice and a celebration of God's faithful provision.

When Balaam was on his way to join the princes of Balak, the angel of the Lord blocked the road with awesome presence because Balaam was on a "reckless path." The donkey saw the angel, but Balaam did not until God opened his eyes to the fierce messenger with a drawn sword blocking his passage.

When Gideon — the youngest kid in a family from the weakest clan in Manasseh — was trying to thresh wheat in a winepress to keep the Midianites from taking it, an angel told him to go save Israel himself. Gideon prepared a goat, its broth, and some bread and offered them to the angel, asking for a sign that the angel was real. The angel told him to put the meat and bread on a rack and pour the broth on and all around it. Gideon did. Then with the tip of his staff, the angel touched the meat and bread. A roaring fire exploded from the rock and consumed the food. When the smoke cleared, the angel was gone. The rest of the story — to make a long story short — was that Gideon sprang into action and made a lot of history.

After Elijah had the prophets of Baal slain, Jezebel threatened to do to him what he had done to the evil prophets. Elijah, scared out of his wits, ran for his life and hid exhausted and hungry deep in the desert, where he collapsed under a broom tree and prayed to die. About then an angel showed up, touched his shoulder, and said, "Get up and eat." Elijah looked around, and there by his head were some fresh hot bread and a carafe of water. He ate and drank, then laid down again. But the angel came back like a good Jewish mother. "Eat, eat," the angel said. "You need plenty of energy for this trip." So, like a good Jewish boy, Elijah obeyed and ate again. It was a good thing, too, for that trip turned out to be a forty-day trek to Mount Horeb. By then, he was ready for a good night's sleep (which he finally got in a cave).

Sometimes angels helped people fight their enemies. But there were times the angels of the Lord showed men that angels really don't need armies at all. When the king of Assyria mocked the God of the Israelites in a letter, Hezekiah showed the letter to God and prayed with all his heart, "O Lord, God of Israel, you alone are God over all the earth. Deliver us so that all kingdoms on earth may know that you alone are God." God answered Hezekiah's prayer with an amazing poem He sent Isaiah the prophet to deliver.

That night, God sent the angel of the Lord to the Assyrian camp, and when morning dawned, eighty-five thousand Assyrians lay dead in the camp. The swaggering King Sennacherib went home to Nineveh, where, while he was in the pagan temple worshiping some god named Nisroch, his own sons cut him down with a sword.

It was a strong and mighty angel who wrestled with Jacob all night long, leaving the usurper of Esau's birthright with a limp. This marked him his whole life as a man willing to fight for a blessing and an identity from God.

It was anything but a wispy creature in feathers that scared Zechariah senseless when he showed up to make an announcement. Barren Elizabeth would give birth to a son he should call John, a son who would be the forerunner of the Messiah.

Only six months later, an awesome creature named Gabriel made a similar visit to Elizabeth's teenage cousin, Mary, telling her she had been chosen to bear the Son of God. For the next couple of years, Gabriel and his squadron were pretty busy shocking shepherds and getting Joseph to relocate.

The Roman soldiers who were assigned to make sure no one stole the body of Jesus after he was crucified were pretty tough guys. But they certainly were no match for the two-angel regiment which flexed their muscles and removed a boulder from the mouth of the tomb so the risen Lord could walk on out. There the two sat, just leaning on their pinions, when the women arrived with embalming spices. When the women found the gaping tomb with no body in it, they came out so blinded by tears that they couldn't tell angels from gardeners. But the angels graciously set them straight and sent them off to tell Peter and the other disciples that Jesus was alive.

That wasn't the last time Peter was to encounter heavenly emissaries. A few years later he was in prison because of his powerful testimony about the living Christ. He was in iron shackles, chained between two guards and sound asleep. The night sentries, however, were not. Suddenly, the dark cell was flooded with light. Peter was awakened by a sharp slap on the side from an angel who said, "Quick, get up!" The iron chains broke and fell off Peter's wrists. "Get dressed, put your coat on, and follow me," said the angel. Peter didn't argue. He thought he was dreaming. Not until they had walked past two more pairs of stunned guards, through an iron gate that swung open before them, and on down a deserted street did Peter realize that he was wide awake and standing alone, liberated from Herod's clutches by an angel of the Lord. At that point, he decided to go on to an all-night prayer meeting at Mary's house; but wouldn't you know it, the servant girl Rhoda who came to the door thought he was a ghost and wouldn't let him in. Peter practically had to wake the neighborhood with his knocking before he could convince the houseful of friends that he was, indeed, not only real but free.

There are other angel sightings in the Scriptures, but these are quite enough to let us know that these ministers of the Lord are much more substantial and powerful, real and purposeful, than our modern press would lead us to believe. Indeed, some of today's so-called angel visitations sound a great deal like the deceptions of Satan that the apostle Paul predicted would appear and make fools of us in the last days.

But we can be confident that there are awesome angels commanded by God to take care of His children and our children. Most of the time the scales of humanness that cover our eyes keep us from seeing the servants of the Lord that protect, prevent, guard, guide, and intercept us every day. These angels are certainly not wispy, weak embellishments for our fireplace mantels; they are mighty, invincible, and swift. They will at the close of time divide the sheep from the goats and harvest God's planting from the tares of evil with a swift and accurate sickle. They will run a number of final missions, as described in Revelation. Angels will stand in the sun calling in a loud voice to all the birds of the air to gather and eat the flesh of kings, generals, mighty men, and all people small and great who rejected the living God (Rev. 19:17–18). Angels will also usher the flawless bride of Christ down the aisle of the holy city that will descend from heaven into the presence of her waiting Groom (Rev. 21:9–27).

In the meantime, we can rest assured that our little children and the innocent of the world have specially assigned angels who report directly to God (Matt. 18:10) and that each of us who have accepted the salvation of our Lord Jesus are surrounded by angels assigned by God (Heb. 1:14; Ps. 91:11) to minister in ways we can only imagine.

Real angels will always accomplish their mission: to make us more clearly see the Lord Jesus and to prevent Satan from attempting to destroy God's family.

Then Came Morning

They all walked away,
Nothing to say;
They'd just lost their dearest friend.
All that He said,
Now He was dead;
So this was the way it would end.

The dreams they had dreamed
Were not what they seemed
Now that He was dead and gone.
The garden, the jail,
The hammer, the nails —
How could a night be so long?

> Then came the morning
> Night turned into day
> The stone was rolled away
> Hope rose with the dawn
> Then came the morning
> Shadows vanished before the Son
> Death had lost and life had won
> For morning had come

The angels, the star,
The kings from afar,
The wedding, the water, the wine —
And now it was done;
They'd taken His Son
Wasted before His time.

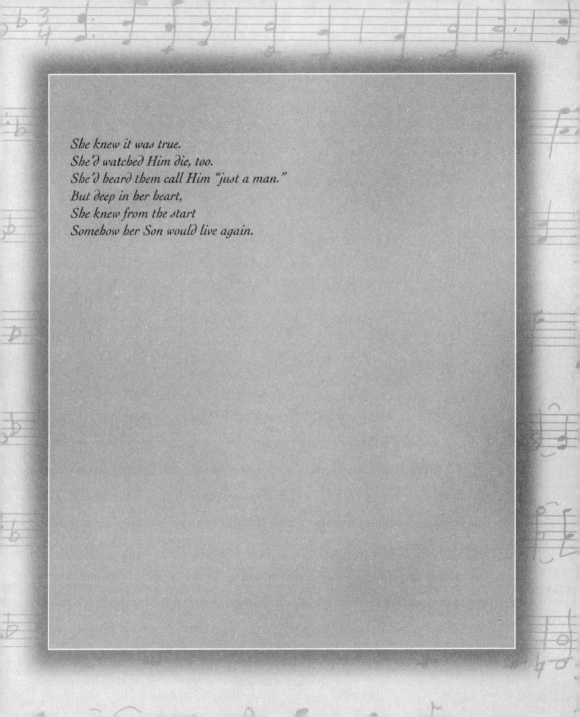

She knew it was true.
She'd watched Him die, too.
She'd heard them call Him "just a man."
But deep in her heart,
She knew from the start
Somehow her Son would live again.

Then Came Morning

At first, after a death, there are things to do: arrangements to make, friends bringing condolences to receive, stories to tell. But after the funeral and burial, reality sets in. The sympathizers go back to their work and lives. The flowers lie wilting on the grave. The leftover casseroles are scraped into the garbage disposal. The house is empty.

Bits and fragments associated with the one so recently present begin the long caravan of reminders: a pair of gardening shoes by the back steps, an old wool plaid coat in the hall closet with a wadded-up tissue and a pack of Clove gum in the pocket, a scribbled note in the margins of a favorite book, a roll of half-exposed film still in the camera, a layaway slip with only half of the payments recorded in the pocket of a worn leather wallet. As the days go by, the other reminders lie in ambush: a fragment of a song on a passing car's radio, an old joke overheard in the grocery store, the smell of a certain kind of fragrance. As Emily Dickinson once wrote, "the sweeping up the heart and putting love away" is the "saddest of all industries enacted upon earth."

Grieving is the private thing after the public ceremonies surrounding a death are over, and no two people do it alike. Some drop out of sight, avoid human contact. Some are terrified of being alone and surround themselves with people. Some treasure a loved one's possessions; others clean them out and move to a new setting not so laden with memories. Some need to talk again and again through the memories and the emotions that go with them. Others clam up and act as if nothing has happened.

We don't know exactly how those who walked with Jesus processed the public execution of their gentle Friend. We do know that one of His friends, a wealthy man named Joseph from a nearby town called Arimathea, went to Pilate and asked to have Jesus' body released to him after it was taken down from the cross. Joseph was an official of the

Jewish Council and had enough status to make the request. We know, too, that Joseph had already purchased the linen shroud and that he wrapped Jesus' body himself and placed it in his own tomb carved in a rock.

We know that everything had to be finished before sundown that strange surreal night because nothing remotely like work or preparations could be done on the Sabbath. But after sundown, how did these very different personalities deal with the reality of Jesus' death? There were John, the gentle lover; Peter, the impetuous; Thomas, the cynic; Mary Magdalene, the much forgiven; Luke, the scientific processor; Salome, the doer; young Mark, the observer of detail; and Mary, the overprotective mother of James. Each must have had a unique reaction.

The Sabbath was a day of required rest, but did they wait in silence? Did they meet at each other's homes and talk it all through? Who first felt rage at the wasteful loss of this man? Who sifted through events for some clue that would make sense of it all, give some logic to this spiral of circumstances? Who of them was in denial, wondering if it had all been a horrible nightmare from which they might awaken any moment?

For the doers, the sunset on that Saturday night released them to get busy. Three of these were Mary Magdalene; Mary, James' mother; and Salome. Preparing spices gave them a practical way to work out their grief, and preparing Jesus' body would let them do something to show their deep love for this Friend who was now gone. Had any one of them caught His line to the Pharisees about restoring "this temple in three days"? Were any of them secretly wondering if, by some act of the Divine, He would return to them? Which of them felt despair?

One thing is certain: nothing halts the grieving process like a resurrection!

This Could Be the Dawning of That Day

A parade began at Calvary;
The saints of all the ages fill its ranks.
O'er the sands of time they're marching to their King's great coronation,
And this could be the dawning of that day!

Nothing here holds their allegiance;
They're not bound by shackles forged of earthly gold.
Since that day they knelt at Calvary they've been
        pilgrims ever wand'ring,
Just looking for a place to rest their souls.

        Oh, this could be the dawning of that grand and glorious day,
        When the face of Jesus we behold!
        Dreams and hopes of all the ages are waiting His returning,
        And this could be the dawning of that day!

All the saints are getting restless;
Oh, what glorious expectation fills each face!
Dreams and hopes of all the ages are awaiting His returning,
And this could be the dawning of that day!

This Could Be the Dawning of That Day

We think about it most during a national crisis. It's then we hear people speculating about the end of the world and which events point to the close of time as we know it.

Bill and I have experienced several such crisis moments. We remember, for instance, the bombing of Hanoi and the escalation of the Vietnam War.

When I was in college, the whole country held its breath during the Cuban Missile Crisis, waiting to see whether nuclear weapons would be deployed (intentionally or by accident) in a moment of intense international pressure.

The Gulf War, because its modern, more destructive means of warfare could ignite the oil fields of the Middle East and blow us all to kingdom come, made us speculate about end-times prophecies. We could see how the battle of Armageddon with soldiers on horseback and hand-to-hand combat might actually occur in this war.

More than once in the last several decades, the bombing raids on Lebanon or the terrorist attacks in Syria, the Golan Heights, or Tel Aviv had us scurrying to Daniel and the book of Revelation for details that might match those on the evening news.

Then the next thing we knew, the explosions from terrorist attacks were not somewhere else but in Oklahoma City, New York, or aboard an airliner on which someone we knew could have been scheduled to fly.

By the end of the twentieth century, the earth itself seemed to have become weary. Pollution and the irresponsible use of her resources had stretched this generous planet to its limits. Like a body aging, the earth now inches its way toward the time when, like a spirit escaping the worn-out encasement that held it, those inhabitants with homes established elsewhere will fly away, leaving the artifact they once used to turn to dust and blow away. We can sense it. Soon, like a pod that holds a seed, the planet could explode — break open and disintegrate — having outlived its usefulness.

No wonder denial and despair are epidemic in our culture. For those who have invested everything in the disintegrating things of earth, these are desolate and desperate times.

But there is excitement in the air for the people of God. The promise we feel in our bones is like the thrill of the countdown for a launch to the moon! Every world event encourages a letting go of stuff and a laying hold of the hope that is within us. The darker the world gets, the brighter burns the hope.

The society of earth has come to "regard waiting as a form of impotence," as author Robin Meyers has phrased it in his book *Morning Sun on a White Piano*. "Do something," he points out, is always the theme of a desperate people. But for those who have "a home not made with hands, eternal in the heavens," life is only "a trip, not a destination." We live, as Meyers puts it, knowing that hope is "the one disposition for which there is no alternative."[1]

We have always been "pilgrims ever wandering, just looking for a place to rest our souls." Our home, our hiding place, has never been

---

[1] Quotations from *Morning Sun on a White Piano*. Written by Dr. Robin R. Meyers. Published by Doubleday (a division of Bantam Doubleday Dell Publishing Group, Inc.). © Copyright 1998 Dr. Robin R. Meyers. All rights reserved. Used by permission.

the edifices of earth, though while we are here, we have taken up temporary residence in them. No, the Lord Himself has been and will always be our safe hiding place, our rock to build a life upon. If the planets disintegrate, He alone will be our trustworthy shield.

As the psalmist said, "Thou art my hiding-place and my shield: I hope in thy word.... Uphold me according unto thy word, that I may live; and let me not be ashamed of my hope" (Ps. 119:114, 116 ASV). So instead of depression, our lives are filled with an exciting sense of urgency. In the place of despair, our hope burns brighter and will until the need for hope is replaced by the incredible reality of a new day dawning.

We find ourselves standing where we always hoped we might stand — out in the wide open spaces of God's grace and glory, standing tall and shouting our praise.

There's more to come: we continue to shout our praise even when we're hemmed in with troubles, because we know how troubles can develop passionate patience in us, and how that patience in turn forges the tempered steel of virtue, keeping us alert for whatever God will do next.

ROMANS 5:2–4 MESSAGE

Yes! And amen.

Part Three

❧◉❧

Lest we become complacent about the miracle of the commonplace, the marvel of the regular, God gives us the refreshing rain of children. Their clean, unjaded insights pull us back from the brink of adult cynicism and call us to recognize and embrace those things that last ... forever.

I Am a Promise

I am a promise; I am a possibility.
I am a promise with a capital P;
I am a great big bundle of potentiality.
And I am learnin' to hear God's voice and I am tryin'
        To make the right choices;
I am a promise to be anything God wants me to be.

Spoken: Hey, you know what? It doesn't matter who you are, or where you live, or who your daddy is, or what you look like! What do you look like? Are you tall, short? Are you fat, skinny? Got holes in your tennis shoes? Freckles on your face? It doesn't matter one bit! You can be anything God wants you to be! And He has something very special in mind for you! It might be climbing mountains, crossing the sea, helping the sick get well, or singing! Whatever it is, you can do it! And don't forget:

I am a promise; I am a possibility.
I am a promise with a capital P;
I am a great big bundle of potentiality.
And I am learnin' to hear God's voice and I am tryin'
        To make the right choices;
I'm a promise to be anything God wants me to be.

I can go anywhere that He wants me to go;
I can be anything that He wants me to be;
I can climb the high mountain; I can cross the wide sea;
I'm a great big promise you see!

        I am a promise to be anything God wants me to be!

I Am a Promise

It started as a song for children, more specifically for our children. It was a song to help them realize that they were full of potential and that God had special expectations for them He wanted to help them realize.

We wrote it full of big words because children love big words, love to feel them roll around in their mouths and then come spilling out into the air, a complete and formed sound with meaning.

But now these nearly thirty years and hundreds of kids later (not all ours, thankfully!), we're beginning to wonder if this was just a kids' song after all.

We've heard stories from young mothers who found hope in remembering that putting their careers on hold to shape an eternal soul is well worth the sacrifice.

Fathers who stayed with not-so-exciting jobs to send kids through college have found encouragement in knowing that job and vocation are not necessarily the same thing.

Women widowed too soon have heard this song on some child's tape player and been reminded that there is no timer on potential and that God always has more — always more — for us to become.

Even nursing home residents have written us to say they are discovering that God still has some promises to keep to the world through their lives, through their prayers, through their ministry of encouragement to those "on the front line."

Truth be known, Bill and I are still discovering what promises God made to the world when each of us was born and what unmined potential remains. Most days we wonder what we're going to be when we grow up and what possibilities are yet to be uncovered.

Children may be rambunctious and awkward. Teenagers may be beleaguered with hormones. Adults may be discovering that the pull of gravity is downward, and golden-agers may be wishing they could unload their bodies altogether because those bodies may be "fumbling" on them. Maybe we're all coming to believe that it isn't about the container at all; it's about the contents — the treasure inside. And that treasure is "Christ in you, the hope of glory" (Col. 1:27). *That* is the promise. You and I hold the promise — we are the promise if we hold Him.

We'll Be There

We'll be there
When you sleep through the night.
We'll be there,
When you need us to hold you tight.
For the first step you take,
And the first time you make it
Clear to the top of the stairs.
When you learn who you are,
When you wish on a star,
We'll be there.

We'll be there
When your words turn to rhyme.
We'll be there
Read you stories at bedtime.
When you play in the park,
When you're scared of the dark,
When you learn how to pray your first prayer.
Through the thunder and storm,
When it's cold or it's warm,
We'll be there.

We'll be there
When you skin up your knees.
We'll be there
When you climb to the top of the trees.
We will teach you to hike,
Ride a two-wheeled bike,
Build a kite that will soar in the air.
When you wade in the streams,
When you dream your first dreams,

We'll be there.

We'll be there
When you try out your wings.
We'll be there
When you're questioning ev'rything.
When you learn how to choose,
When you try and you lose,
And you find that the world is unfair.
When you stand or you fall,
You can know through it all,
We'll be there.

We'll be there
When you think you're alone.
We'll be there,
Pro'bly waiting to use the phone!
When you're out on a date
And you get home too late,
And you quietly slip up the stairs,
Though you might never guess,
We're awake; we won't rest
'Till you're there.

We'll be there
When you're out on your own.
We'll be there
So proud of the way you've grown.
Thanking God ev'ry day
That He sent you our way,
And He trusted you once to our care.
And wherever you roam,
You can always come home;
We'll be there.

We'll Be There

There's a sign on our kitchen wall that was hung when our children were in middle school and I was the car pool champion of Madison County. It says, "If a woman's place is in the house, what am I doing in the car?"

I liked that sign for several reasons. For one, it pokes fun at the stupid idea that any healthy person, regardless of gender, should stay in the house! For another, it snickers at the shallow idea that a woman's role as lover, mate, parent, and home-nurturer could possibly be defined in terms of running a vacuum cleaner, starting a dishwasher, folding clothes, and baking cookies.

I thought I would take the sign down when the kids all got their driver's licenses. But alas, I still need it to give me hope, because now our house is alive with a new crop of children — our children's children and their buddies. I now drive a seven-passenger utility vehicle because a nice "grandmotherly sedan" won't hold enough car seats or provide enough seat belts for those days I have all four grandkids at once.

I'm still often in the car when we're not all digging in the garden, fishing in the creek, painting on the sidewalk, or having peanut butter and jelly sandwiches in the tree house. Bill and I are still gone a lot, traveling together or separately. We all love the house but discovered long ago that "being there" for each other had a broader meaning than just being in the house.

Amy, for instance, is an actress. She's always been an actress, even long before she finished her master of fine arts degree at the University of Nebraska and became a pro at what she loves. Being there for her has included traveling to performances all over the country, raiding the house for props and costumes, and now, helping juggle their children when she and Andrew are both involved in productions.

Being present to Benjy has meant late night discussions about song ideas, career aspirations, and long-term dreams. It has taken us on fishing trips and to rock concerts. It has made me a student of animation techniques, basketball plays, and guitar "licks."

Suzanne and I took our graduate classes in English together and spent Monday nights eating Chinese food and discussing Melville. We are there for each other when we read a great paragraph of a novel, find a fresh metaphor in a poem, or think of a "hook" worth hanging a new song on.

Bill and I once thought of parenting as those years when children are between birth and eighteen and are living under the parents' roof. We have since learned that kids don't leave; they multiply. And parenting is a lifelong assignment and privilege. We learned that truth not from our children but from our parents. They were there for us until they died and are still parenting us with the wisdom and example they taught us.

We have learned that the sleep deprivation we experience when our babies have their days and nights confused and colic rules the digestive system is nothing compared to the sleepless nights brought on by our children's "dark night of the soul" or the churning in our own digestive tract from not knowing where our children are in their pilgrimage of the spirit.

We have learned that prayer isn't the last resort when we're out of answers. It is our *only* recourse that lets us miraculously rest in the knowing that He is answer enough.

We have learned that the best thing we can give our children is our love for each other and our commitment in the deep valleys of life to be there till death do us part.

Over, around, beside, and under everything is the promise of God to be there for us all. "I will never leave thee, nor forsake thee" (Heb. 13:5 KJV) are some of the sweetest words ever written. And they were spoken by the one person who ever lived and only told the truth.

For us who pledge to be family to each other, being there may mean being apart, being in prayer, being on call, being patient to wait, or simply being willing to stay. It often means being in pain. And would you believe it? Sometimes it means staying in the house baking cookies.

God Loves to Talk to Little Boys While They're Fishin'

God loves to talk to little boys while they're fishin';
That seems to be the time boys listen best.
It's the only quiet time there is for wishin';
It's the only time when God and boys can rest.

A boy can hear God's whisper in the willow,
His laughter in the babbling of the brook.
God understands the fun there is in fishin',
The joy of finding something on your hook.

There's somethin' 'bout a boy who's good at fishin';
God knows he'll make a very special friend.
A boy who learns to listen while he's fishin'
Can hear God when it's time to fish for men.

God loves to talk to little boys while they're fishin';
That seems to be the time boys listen best.
It's the only quiet time there is for wishin';
It's the only time when God and boys can rest.

God Loves to Talk to Little Boys While They're Fishin'

They were the three ragamuffins of the neighborhood — undisciplined and usually unsupervised. We were surprised to see them at our door when the doorbell rang, standing there with fishing rods and a couple of tin cans full of earthworms.

"Mr. Gaither, would it be all right if we fished in your creek?" I heard them ask. Bill began to explain that we had made a place down by the highway for kids to fish outside the fence.

"Yes, we know," one of them interrupted. "We've fished there, but we haven't caught anything. Please, we promise we won't bother the swans. Just for a while, can we fish in the big pond? Please?"

I was a little surprised when I heard Bill give his consent and a few instructions. "Don't chase the geese and swans, don't go near their nests, and be sure to take all your empty bait containers with you when you leave."

They won't last long down there, I thought as we watched the boys run down the hillside and settle under the big willow tree. *They have short attention spans unless they're getting into trouble.*

We were working on a song that morning at the piano in the family room, so we were too absorbed to notice the boys for a couple of hours. Finally, Bill caught sight of a little red cap bobbing along the creek bank.

"Those kids are still down there, honey," he said. "They've hardly moved since they started fishing. What is it about little boys and fishing?"

Images of my mother teaching our son to fish filled my mind. She had taught me to fish, too, and to love the sound of water slapping against the old wooden rowboat, the mesmerizing motion of the bobber floating along with the current, the sound of loons calling to their mates.

My reverie was interrupted by the sound of the piano; Bill had begun to tinker with a simple tune. I picked up my yellow tablet and began to write some words that seemed to fit the melody: "God loves to talk to little boys while they're fishin'. It seems to be the time boys listen best. . . ."

"I'll bet that's the longest those kids have gone all week without getting yelled at," Bill said.

"And the longest they've been still in a month," I answered.

The song was recorded on our second kids' project, called *I Am a Promise,* by the Gaither Trio and the Sunday School Picnic (the name we gave the children who sang with us). Since then the song has been sung by kids all over the country. It has been recorded and arranged many times, including the classic video performance by George Younce and Madison Easter on *The Homecoming Kids Camp Out* video.

Sometimes we get letters from little girls who like to fish, too, as I did growing up around Michigan lakes. We assure them that neither fishing nor listening to God are gender exclusive. It's just that the song was inspired by three roughneck little boys who spent a very quiet morning one Saturday fishing in Gaither's Pond.

> *There's somethin' 'bout a boy who's good at fishin';*
> *God knows he'll make a very special friend.*
> *A boy who learns to listen while he's fishin'*
> *Can hear God when it's time to fish for men.*

I Wish You

I wish you some springtime,
Some "bird on the wing" time
For blooming and sending out shoots;
I wish you some test time,
Some winter and rest time
For growing and putting down roots.
I wish you some summer,
For you're a becomer,
With blue skies and flowers and dew;
For there is a reason
God sends ev'ry season:
He's planted His image in you.

I wish you some laughter,
Some "happy thereafter"
To give you a frame for your dreams;
But I wish you some sorrows,
Some rainy tomorrows,
Some clouds with some sun in between.
I wish you some crosses,
I wish you some losses,
For only in losing you win.
I wish you some growing,
I wish you some knowing,
There's always a place to begin.

We'd like to collect you
And shield and protect you
And save you from hurts if we could;
But we must let you grow tall

To learn and to know all
That God has in mind for your good.
We never could own you,
For God only loaned you
To widen our world and our hearts.
So we wish you His freedom,
Knowing where He is leading;
There is nothing can tear us apart.

I Wish You

It was our daughter Suzanne's graduation party. Family and friends and relations, schoolmates and former teachers gathered near the creek under the big willow to sip punch and eat raspberry cake. Suzanne opened the lovely gifts piled on the table in the gazebo. This is the place where she had played when she was a child. She had spent many a summer day fishing in the creek and catching turtles and garter snakes. Our family had built many a bonfire in this place for roasting hot dogs and marshmallows. When she started dating, it was by this creek that Suzanne had walked with her boyfriends, watching the sunset.

Memories raced across the green hillside and peeped out from behind the apple trees in the orchard. Bill and I listened as our friends wished our daughter success as a writer, fame as a lyricist, fortune in her chosen work, and honors in graduate school.

After the party was over and the guests had gone their separate ways, Bill and I sat in the yard swing. *What would we wish her?* we asked ourselves. It wouldn't be wealth, we decided, or notoriety. And success is hard to define. We wouldn't wish her failure, but we knew that sometimes we learn more from our failures than from our successes. And we had seen wealth destroy some people yet be used by others to bless and encourage.

We hoped she would continue to grow in her knowledge of Christ Jesus, just as she had right before our eyes through the years since she first committed her life to Him. Yes, we would wish her growth, knowing full well that would require some sunshine and rain, successes and failures, joy and pain.

We would wish her insight and a clear sense of direction. We would wish her the ability to sense when others hurt and the compassion to do something about it whenever she could. We would wish her, most of all, what Paul had hoped for those he had come to love in the new church at Ephesus. This passage had come to be very important to us in our home, and now as we tried to express what we were feeling as parents, it seemed to best express our hearts:

> *When I think of the wisdom and scope of his plan I fall down on my knees and pray to the Father of all the great family of God . . . that out of his glorious, unlimited resources he will give you the mighty inner strengthening of his Holy Spirit. And I pray that Christ will be more and more at home in your hearts, living within you as you trust in him. May your roots go down deep into the soil of God's marvelous love; and may you be able to feel and understand, as all God's children should, how long, how wide, how deep, and how high his love really is; and to experience this love for yourselves, though it is so great that you will never see the end of it or fully know or understand it. And so at last you will be filled up with God himself.*

> *EPHESIANS 3:14–19 LB*

We wanted to shield her from anything that might hurt her, yet we knew we could never insulate her from the world. The wisest choice was to dare to entrust her to the care of the Lord, who had made her in the first place and who loves her more perfectly than we ever could.

Some Things I Must Tell the Children

How can we tell you the things we must tell you,
The things that we want you to know —
All about living and reasons for giving
And things that will help you to grow?
Oh, we've watched your diet, taught you to be quiet
In places of worship and school;
We've kept you well groomed with a nice, tidy room,
And we've mentioned the Golden Rule.

But along the way did your heart hear us say
That you don't have to earn our love?
Not a thing you could do could make us stop loving you;
Just the joy that you've brought is enough.
There isn't a thing that the future could bring
That could take back the gift that you are;
You are a treasure we never could measure —
Just some things we must tell the children.

I'm sure we've told you to mind all your manners
And to get to appointments on time;
And we remind you to hang up your clothes
And finish the homework assigned.
You've learned to care for your teeth and your hair,
And you make your own bed every day;
You got decent grades, and your lunch money's paid,
And you won your first game yesterday.

But did we make it clear; were you able to hear,
As you skipped through the house and our lives,
That God has a plan that you must understand
No matter how much you "arrive"?

Never stop dreaming, keep working and singing,
But remember just Whose child you are;
Stand tall and walk straight, and be home before eight —
Just some things we must tell the children.

And whatever you do, remember: we love you —
Just some things we must tell the children.

Some Things I Must Tell the Children

~

Every day a busy household is filled with instructions and activity. We watch our own daughters now going through the frantic busyness of a new day full of young children's routines, husbands' career needs, their own schedules of work and ministry, and the demands of household management. Post-it Notes are everywhere, as they were in our own kitchen, bathroom, and car.

Water softener repairman — 10:30 Tues.

Will's piano lessons Wed. after school

Check Madeline's cast — Dr. apt. 9:30 Mon.

Pick up Jesse and Lee from soccer Thurs.

11:45 — Meet Suzanne for lunch

Barry in Nashville Mon. night. Pick up at airport 10:00 pm

Grandma's birthday — dinner Saturday at Olive Garden

All day long young parents are reminding, encouraging, instructing, rebuking, then reminding some more! Take your vitamins. Don't forget your lunch money. Tie your shoes. Brush your teeth. Make your bed. Where's your jacket? Got an umbrella? Time to practice! Time to eat. Time to go to bed. Hey! Wake up, sleepyhead. Time for school! Don't forget to feed the dog.

The other morning I answered the phone. It was Suzanne. "Mom," she said, "could you pick up Jesse and give him a nap at your house so I can finish this song?"

"Sure. Be happy to," I answered. "We'll get lunch. I have three new books we'll read, and I'll be glad for an excuse to stop myself."

I remembered all the times my mother picked up our kids or Bill's parents fixed them supper when I was trying to carve out a few hours to myself to write a lyric or work with Bill on an idea that had been incubating in our minds.

So many nights of our lives, Bill and I have fallen into bed exhausted, our backs throbbing from fatigue. In the dark we would reach for each other's hands and try to remember what we had done that day to make us so tired. Appointments and music lessons, ball games and play practices, meetings and lunch dates paraded across our minds. "But was there any eternity in it?" one of us would ask the other. To tell you the truth, sometimes it would be hard to find, in all the activities of the day, one or two with any lasting significance.

Out of that question came a song we wrote to remind us to teach something that had some eternity in it. In the winter of 1986 — our children were fifteen, sixteen, and twenty — I wrote in my journal some messages I hoped we had communicated, not just with our mouths but with our lives, in answer to the self-imposed question, "What do we want to give our children?"

We want to give our children the gift of solitude, the gift of knowing the joy of silence, the chance to be alone and not feel uncomfortable. We want to give them transportation for the inner journey and water for their desert places. We want to make them restless with diversion and disenchanted with the excesses of our culture. We want to give them a desire to strip life to its essentials and the courage to embrace whatever they find there.

We would teach our children to be seers, to notice subtleties in nature and people and relationships. We long for them to grasp the meaning of things, to hear the sermons of the seasons, the exhortations of the universe, the warnings of the wounded environment.

We would teach them to listen. It would bring us joy to happen in on them and find them with their hearts to the earth or humming the melody of the meadow or dancing to the music of the exploding symphony of spring.

Yes, we would teach them to dance! We would teach them never to so tie up their feet with responsibility that they can't whirl to the rhythm of the spheres. We would have them embrace the lonely, sweep children into their arms, give wings to the aged, and dance across the barriers of circumstance, buoyed by humor and imagination into the ecstasy of joy. We would teach them to dance!

We would teach our children to cry, to feel the pain that tears at the violated, to sense the emptiness of the deserted, to hear the plaintive call of the disoriented, and to understand the hopelessness of the powerless. We would teach them to cry — for what is locked away or broken, for what was not realized, for those who never knew Life, for the least and the last to know freedom.

We would teach our children gratitude. We would give them the gift of knowing where they've been and who brought them where they are. We would teach them to write each day a liturgy in praise of what is, not waste their energies on what could have been.

And we would have them know that twin of gratitude, contentment. We would have them be content to live and breathe, to love and be loved, to have shelter and sustenance, to know wonder, to be able to think and feel and see. To always call a halt to senseless striving — this we would teach our children.

We would teach our children integrity, to be truthful at any cost, to be bound by their word, to make honest judgments even against themselves, to be just, to have pure motives. We would have them realize that they are accountable individually to God and to themselves. We would have them choose right even if it is not popular or understood — even by us.

We would teach our children to pray, knowing that in our relationship with God there is much to be said and that God is the one who must say it. We would have them know the difference between prayer and piety and make them aware that prayer often has no words but only an open, vulnerable accessibility to God's love, mercy, grace, and justice.

We would hope they discover that prayer is an awareness of our need, an awareness necessary for all growing and becoming. We would have our children know through experience and example that there is nothing too insignificant to lay before God. And yet we would have them learn that often when we come to Him, He lifts us up until the matter we brought before Him seems insignificant compared with the revelation He brings to us.

We would not have our children think of prayer as a commercial enterprise, a sort of celestial clearinghouse for distributing earth's material goods. Rather, we would have prayer teach them that what we think we seek so often is not on the list of what we need, that God does not upbraid us for our seeking but delights in our coming to Him, even when we don't understand.

Mostly we would have our children know how synonymous true prayer is with gratitude and contentment and have them discover the marvelous outlet prayer provides for communicating this delight with God.

Last, we would teach our children to soar, to rise above the common yet find delight in the commonplace, to fly over the distracting disturbances of life yet see from this perspective ways to attack the knotty problems that thwart people's growth and stymie their development. We would give them wings to dream and insight to see beyond the now, and we would have those wings develop strength from much use, so others may be borne aloft as well when life becomes too weighty for them to bear.

At last these wings, we know, will take our children high and away from our reach to places we have together dreamed of. And we will watch and cheer as they fade from our view into vistas grand and new, and we will be glad.[1]

---

[1]From *Moments to Remember*. Written by Gloria Gaither. © Copyright 1988 by Gloria Gaither. All rights reserved.

I Have Seen the Children

I have never climbed a mountain,
Sailed the surf off Waikiki,
Ridden horseback down the canyon,
Never sailed the seven seas,
Never camped out in the Tetons,
Seen a Black Hills Passion Play,
Watched Old Faithful in the sunset,
Walked the islands in the bay.

> Oh, but I have seen the children —
> Black and yellow, white and brown;
> And I've felt their arms around me —
> Heard them laugh and watched them frown.
> And I've listened to their parents,
> Had them look me in the eye —
> "Bring the music; don't forget us;
> Desert days are hot and dry.
> And sometimes the heart's a desert
> And the music is the rain —
> Bring the singing; send the music;
> Won't you come our way again?"

In Nova Scotia there's a lighthouse
Rising from the jagged rocks.
And in London there's a craftsman
Who hand-makes a perfect clock.
In South Tucson is a cowboy
Who can rope the wildest steer.
In Seattle there's an artist
Painting saw blades on the pier.

But what I have seen are windows
Looking out on parking lots —
Dressing rooms and motel lobbies,
Airport gates and night truck stops.
Backstage gray and green arenas
And their hollow, empty space
Changed into a great cathedral
By some miracle of grace;
When ten thousand, three, or twenty
Gather there to praise His name,
There's no sight earth has to offer
That can rival such a place.

And I have seen the children —
Black and yellow, white and brown;
And I've felt their arms around me —
Heard them laugh and watched them frown.
And I've listened to their parents,
Had them look me in the eye —
"Bring the music; don't forget us;
Desert days are hot and dry.
And sometimes the heart's a desert
And the music is the rain —
Bring the singing; send the music;
Won't you come our way again?"

I Have Seen the Children

Most songs come to Bill and me from the "daily" of our lives. Perhaps this is because a philosophy of life has to work on regular days if it is to serve in a crisis.

For thirty years I have kept a journal, and I believe that everyone could benefit from this eye-opening practice. Journaling has taught me that the things we think are so important often turn out to be no big deal. And what we think is so insignificant that it's barely worth recording often turns out to be the very thing that produces eternal insights into life itself. Someone has said there are no insiginificant choices; the destiny of our days often hinges on a routine decision.

While our children were small, Bill and I traveled only on weekends so we could be normal parents during the week. Often we would take one of our children with us so we could give the child who seemed to need it most our undivided attention for the whole weekend. The other two stayed home with my parents. But later, after Suzanne reached junior high school, we chose to stay home most weekends and take two or three tours a year that would last about two weeks. These times seemed very long to us, but this arrangement allowed us to be home for our kids' ball games, concerts, and other activities.

During one such tour in the fall of 1981, I made an entry in my journal that, later on, inspired a song. This is the entry:

October 1 — on the road: I find I have to put my mind in some special kind of neutral to stay away this long. Long absence throws off all my natural chemistry.

The concerts have been excellent, but it is hard to keep enough of my heart here to be complete between concerts. It becomes a circus existence: get up, eat breakfast, read, take a bath, go to early supper, sound check, get ready, do the concert, talk to people, get into the bus, drive all night, and start again.

Interspersed are some lovely moments with the troupe, and often there are wonderful times with Bill. But constant travel takes on an aura of fantasy — like riding a glider, looking for a safe and solid place to land.

I've even taken up embroidery. I'd rather write, but the bus is too bumpy, and my creative energies are drained by the intense exertion of the concerts and the dulling boredom of endless miles.

I would love the miles if there were time to stop and see things, but we're always driven right past the wonders of the world by the tyranny of our schedule. I've been in every state in the Union, yet I've never seen the Grand Canyon, Yellowstone, Yosemite, the Tetons, Glacier National Park, a Black Hills Passion Play, or the islands in Puget Sound.

But I've seen people — and the terrains that mold their temperaments and shape their values. I've sensed the demands made on them by the stubborn rocks or the severity of the climate. I've seen the barren deserts that threaten them and the crowded cities that rob them of their uniqueness. I've seen the wide-open spaces that teach them to trust other human beings, and I've seen the congested neighborhoods that teach them to peer at the world through frightened eyes.

I've touched the children — from Manhattan to Montana, from San Antonio to Saginaw — and I've felt the hope and fear in them. I've watched them reach for me in open affection and shrink from me in distrust. I've seen promises with blond pigtails and black shiny pixies. I've had black and brown, yellow, white, and reddish arms around my neck. With my heart I've learned to understand love in a dozen languages.

I've heard their parents say, "Come to us!" They say it from the seclusion of North Dakota. They say it from the anonymity of the Bronx. They say it from the mountain poverty of Kentucky and from the lighted plastic glitter of Las Vegas.

"Come to us!" they say. "Don't forget us."

As if we could.

"Why do you do it?" the glib reporters ask. I find myself looking into their eyes for some clue to the living person inside the professional — only a person could understand. Otherwise, I don't have the words. I'm sure they'd smile their well-rehearsed, objective, detached smiles and be polite while I say, "'It' is Jesus; He's come to us and given us life. Now we have to go."

They'd nod politely and think "money," "glamour," "travel," "fame," "excitement." They'd only think it was a gimmick if I told them that my mother's heart is pulled apart, my body is exhausted, and my brain is in suspension. They wouldn't believe me if I told them it's the Reason bigger than life, the Place wider than here, the Time beyond the now, and the unforgettable voices rising over millions of miles and fifteen years of days, joining in a deafening chorus that will not go away, "Come to us — don't forget us!"

... And I know I have to go because Someone came to me.

Later, after rereading this entry, I wrote the lyric to "I Have Seen the Children." A wonderful friend, award-winning country songwriter Paul Overstreet, set the lyric to music, and Bill and I recorded it on the *Welcome Back Home* project of the Bill Gaither Trio. It has always served to remind me why we sing, travel, write, and serve and that we must never mistake activity for our true mission in life.

Welcome Back Home

Dear Son,

Can you hear what I'm writing you? Although we've not heard from you since that morning you left the house, there's not been a day we have not watched for you, waited for you, walked by the emptiness of your room.

How I long for you to somehow know, wherever you are, that you're loved and, yes, forgiven, before you even ask. I know that the road you have taken will bring you pain. How can I let you know we hurt with you? I know the way you've chosen will leave you lonely and afraid. In the night, when you have only the empty silence for company, after those who have used you are all gone away, well, you know that you are not alone.

Can you feel how our arms ache to hold you? How our eyes watch the horizon every evening and search the mist of every dawn for the glimpse of your returning. And though I can't send you this letter, it's written on the wind, it's etched in every sunset, it's whispered by the grasses of the field. No matter how far away you go, you are our son, and nothing you can do, no distance or choice, will make us stop loving you.

Silence hid the anger
As he took his promised pay;
He would show them he could make it on his own.
Then seething with resentment,
He turned and walked away
Without a backward glance at what he'd known.

> *And hurt was in the silence*
> *As he watched him fade from view,*
> *This son who'd brought him laughter, joy, and tears.*
> *And thus began the waiting,*
> *The years without a word,*
> *The praying that someday he'd reappear.*

My son, I love you;
You are forgiven.
You still belong here;
Won't you come home?
The fam'ly's waiting
To celebrate you.
You are forgiven;
Won't you come home?

A figure in the distance
Is etched against the sky —
A house, black-silhouetted on the hill —
A father stops — suspended —
Oh, could it be his son?
The son walks resolutely through the chill.

The distance now is shortened
'Tween father and the son;
The jolt of recognition slows their pace.
The paralyzing question
Hangs silent in the air,
Then a father holds his son in sweet embrace.

My son, I love you;
You are forgiven!
You still belong here;
Welcome back home.
The fam'ly's waiting
To celebrate you!
All is forgiven!
Welcome back home!

Welcome Back Home

~

I've often wondered what the prodigal son's mother was doing all that time her boy was away. The biblical account says the father had been the one who had the confrontation with their son. The young man wanted his inheritance *now*. He wanted to take charge of his own life. He didn't buy the old promise of deferred gratification.

The father must have come back to the bedroom and collapsed on the edge of the bed, his head in his hands, and sobbed as he told the boy's mother that he had given their son his share prematurely and that he was, even as they spoke, packing to leave the house and set out on his own.

He hadn't listened to reason; he hadn't wanted to hear about how much richer he would one day be if he would trust his father to make wise investments for him and, as the inheritance grew, allow his father to teach him everything he would now learn the hard way. No, he wouldn't hear of it. He wanted his share now, not when he was too old to enjoy it, like his father.

How torn that mother must have felt between the practical wisdom of her husband and a mother's need to try to understand, too, where the boy was coming from. He wasn't a bad boy. He was just immature, and she well remembered the passions that once drove this man she loved to take risks, strike out on faith. Hadn't he loved her when she was a naïve and inexperienced girl? What had they known then of what the future would hold?

She could feel her heart splitting down the middle. She was helpless to stop what was happening to her family.

She stood silently with her hand on her husband's heaving shoulder. What could she say? It was done now. The boy was an adult for all intents and purposes, yet in her heart she knew that, protected and provided for as he'd been, he'd be a sheep among wolves once he got wherever he was determined to go. He didn't have a clue!

It was as if that whole evening were moving in slow motion, like the recurring dream she'd had since she was a girl, the dream in which she was trying to run down the lane to her old childhood farmhouse. Something she couldn't see was chasing her and she could feel it gaining on her, but her legs wouldn't work right and she couldn't seem to scream for help. She just kept trying to run or call but couldn't do either. She would wake up in a sweat, unable to identify her fear.

She felt the same panic rise now. It had no face, yet she could almost feel it breathing on the back of her neck. She could only pray that her son would come to his senses before something tragic happened.

The boy left. His parents stood and watched as he slowly turned into a speck on the horizon, then disappeared. They both went back to their routine after that. Thank God for work! But they kept feeling as if there was something pending, that all their sentences ended with question marks.

Their other son kept things going. They could always depend on him, and they were grateful. The farm prices stayed steady. The crops flourished, yet somehow their prosperity and good fortune seemed pointless. The color in their lives was gone, and they moved about through sepia-toned days.

The mother would often catch her husband standing on the porch around sundown, looking at the place on the horizon where their son had disappeared, but he never mentioned how much he missed his son. She longed to talk about the things that gnawed at her heart and churned in her stomach, but her husband was a man of few words and she knew he would respect his son's decision to walk away.

Often at night when the house was still and she could hear everyone's measured breathing, she would slip down the stairs to the bench and table by the window. She would pick up the quill and write letters she knew could never be sent. There was no address for "a far country." Or sometimes she would climb to the roof, where she could see the stars and feel the breeze stirring the night. Here where there was no risk of being heard by the household servants, she would send her son messages on the wind, for it must blow, too, where her son had gone. And she would pray.

Her husband saw him first. He was standing on the porch like he often did at the end of the day, straining toward the horizon. He called to her. Did she see it? That speck where the road met the waning sunset?

At first she saw only the heat waves rising from the freshly plowed field. No, to the right of the clearing — did she see it?

She couldn't dare to hope, yet the figure now materializing was unmistakably a man . . . but her husband was already running down the lane toward the road.

Even So, Lord Jesus, Come

In a world of fear and turmoil,
In a race that seems so hard to run;
Lord, I need Thy rich infilling,
Even so, Lord Jesus, come.

When my eyes shall span the river,
When I gaze into the vast unknown;
May I say with calm assurance,
"Even now, Lord Jesus, come."

Even so, Lord Jesus, come,
My heart doth long for Thee;
Tho I've failed and betrayed Thy trust,
Even so, Lord Jesus, come.

Even So, Lord Jesus, Come

Many of our songs were written when we were very young. I was barely twenty-one when the song "Even So, Lord Jesus, Come" was inspired by the last two verses of the book of Revelation. "He which testifieth these things saith, Surely I come quickly," writes John the Revelator, then adds his very personal response to that promise: "Amen. Even so, come, Lord Jesus" (KJV).

Bill and I thought we understood those verses then and were moved by them to write our own version of "Amen! Come ahead, Lord Jesus." But as is true for many of our songs, there was much more to understand about what God had given us than we knew. Only time and experience could give us the deeper and broader comprehension of the concepts we then were only beginning to grasp.

God used our second child, Amy, who was then not even born, to give us new insight into our own song.

There's a golden time of evening, just before the children sleep, when little people open up their hearts and invite adults to come in. They never let us stay long, only long enough to glimpse their hearts. Who could resist such an opportunity? For the secrets children share at these fleeting moments are indeed rare.

"Mother," five-year-old Amy said to me one evening, after we had snuggled long enough for her to fumble open the door-latch of her heart. "Mother, when we die ... when we die, do we go to heaven or does heaven come to us?"

I waited, trying to judge by inadequate weights and measures the value of this treasure about to be placed in my hands. "I mean, Mommy, do you believe in chariots?"

"The Bible speaks of chariots, honey," I began carefully. "There have been people who said they saw them in visions. I don't know if they saw actual chariots or whether they just chose that word to explain something we have no word to express. Why do you ask?"

"Well, what I really want to know is, does something take us to heaven, or does heaven come to us?" She paused a moment, thinking. Then she said, "It seems to me that being here holds heaven back, but when we die, heaven can just come on in."

The immensity of the room she'd opened to me almost took my breath away. There was little I could say. I mumbled something simple like, "You may be right, dear; you may be right," and I kissed her sleepy eyes. I could feel the door closing gently behind her as she floated off into the world of dreams, but the wonder of the truth she'd let me glimpse remained indelibly imprinted in my mind.

Her insight was so clear, so simple. Of course! It is the limitations of our humanness that shackle us to this time-world — that keep heaven pushed back and away. But when we die, heaven can just come in.

As Amy slept peacefully, I began a lifelong pilgrimage down the path of insight revealed by her words. When we come to Jesus, we begin then to let heaven in. The more we can let go of the earth in us, the more space we can hollow out for the eternal. It's a lifelong process of gradually submitting areas of our lives to the Lord so heaven can come into them. Being tied to this earth by our physical bodies, we will always be separated from the fullness of heaven. We aren't equipped to take it in. We couldn't contain the glory. But when death comes, the containers of earth — these physical vessels — crumble and heaven will come flooding in. Eternity that has begun in our hearts can then completely possess us! What a beautiful simple way to clear up the mystery of heaven! Once again I stood in awe of the wisdom of a child. I had heard great discussions and read impressively difficult theological theories about heaven, but here was a fresh picture — so simple, so obvious. "Out of the mouth of babes . . ." (Ps. 8:2 KJV). "God has chosen the wisdom of the simple to confound the wise" (see 1 Cor. 1:27). It isn't that this life is *here* and heaven is *out there* somewhere beyond the blue. Heaven is all around just waiting for us to recognize it, embrace it.

I thought of all those wonderful times when the Holy Spirit had been so near and His presence so sweet, times when for a few moments we had glimpsed and held a bit of heaven. How satisfying were those tasty morsels, and yet how hungry and thirsty they made us for more. How often we have shared the passion of the psalmist who wrote, "As the hart panteth after the water brooks, so panteth my soul after thee, O God. My soul thirsteth for God, for the living God" (Ps. 42:1–2 KJV). Harts aren't supposed to pant. They pant only when they are deprived of water. And God wants us to drink Him in, in huge satisfying draughts. If we are panting, it is to drive us to the living water — to make us realize that without the living water we will die!

How often after a long spiritual drought, when the shackles of earth had caused us to live by blind and stubborn faith, have Bill and I prayed for those rich, sweet, refreshing times of knowing that heaven is still there, waiting on the outskirts of this time-world to pour in and possess us. How thankful we have been for the assurance that the Comforter has come to lift the veil that holds heaven back and let in enough of it to fill the spaces we have hollowed out with the shovels of our commitment.

Sometimes we have found it difficult to explain to those who have never tasted of eternity the thirst and hunger that drive us to the cool springs and the manna of the Spirit. It wasn't always easy for me to understand the excitement Christians feel about meeting together to feast on the Word or share their songs of praise and joy. But now I know, because I've tasted it for myself, that the greatest riches this world can boast can never compare with one morsel of the good things of the Lord.

Amy was right. Heaven is all around, just waiting to come on in. One day we will fully know the reality to which we have given ourselves in faith here. Paul says it best:

We don't yet see things clearly. We're squinting in a fog, peering through a mist. But it won't be long before the weather clears and the sun shines bright! We'll see it all then, see it all as clearly as God sees us, knowing him directly just as he knows us!

But for right now, until that completeness, we have three things to do to lead us toward that consummation: Trust steadily in God, hope unswervingly, love extravagantly. And the best of the three is love.

1 CORINTHIANS 13:9–13 MESSAGE

Part Four

⟨◯⟩●⟨◯⟩

Just as the wisdom of children refreshes our spirit, maturity of experience gives us perspective. The allure of instant gratification fades in the light of eternal performance as we walk a path that, we learn, does not end at the grave but only widens there and climbs to a new place beyond the pull of the temporary.

Old Friends

A phone call, a letter,
A pat on the back, or a "Hey, I just dropped by to say . . ."
A hand when we're down, a loan when we just couldn't pay —
A song or a story, a rose from the florist, a note that you happened to send —
Out of the blue just to tell us that you're still our friend —

> Old friends — after all of these years, just
> Old friends — through the laughter and tears.
> Old friends — what a find! What a priceless treasure!
> Old friends — like a rare piece of gold.
> Old friends — make it great to grow old.
> 'Till then, through it all I will hold to old friends.

> Oh, God must have known
> There'd be days on our own
> We would lose our will to go on.
> That's why He sent friends like you along.

> Old friends — yes, you've always been there.
> My old friends — we've had more than our share.
> Old friends — I'm a rich millionaire in old friends.

We've been through some tough times
When we didn't know whether we'd even have one thin dime —
But that didn't change you; you stayed by our side the whole time —
When we were big winners and everything seemed to be finally going our way —
You just cheered us on, so glad to be able to say —

> Old friends — after all of these years, just
> Old friends — through the laughter and tears.
> Old friends — what a find! What a priceless treasure!
> Old friends — like a rare piece of gold.
> Old friends — make it great to grow old.
> 'Till then, through it all I will hold to old friends.

Old Friends

*F*riendship is one of the few human experiences that can outlast this life. It is a gift. Long-term friendship is a rare treasure. Much has been written about how to initiate, develop, and maintain friendship. Cute suggestions often include surprises under pillows, notes on the steering wheel, and cards sent on special holidays. But the best kind of friendship often begins quite by accident between not so similar people and develops rather sporadically over time in the daily grind of life.

When forced into the crucible of life, great friendships, as the Skin Horse said in *The Velveteen Rabbit*, "don't have to be carefully kept." No one keeps track of who sent the last letter or who had whom over for dinner. Great friends don't get miffed if you don't call for two days, two weeks, or two months. Whenever you do get to be together, you can just pick up where you left off as if no time has lapsed at all. Yet you know a great friend will be there for you when push comes to shove.

Over the years, you gather a whole collection of times when a friend was there for you or when you saw a friend through a crisis. These occasions become silken threads that, once collected, are woven into strong ties that bind. In the book *Friends for the Journey*, written with her friend Luci Shaw, Madeleine L'Engle writes, "On television we see instant love. But friendship, like all fine things, needs time for ripening. We need to believe in it, knowing that we are all human creatures who make mistakes, even with (or perhaps *especially* with) those we love. We need forbearance and patience and love."[1]

Proverbs says a great deal about friends — how to be one, how to recognize one. A friend is, for one thing, consistent and doesn't "wimp out" when things get uncomfortable. As wise Solomon put it, "A friend loves at all times, and . . . is born for adversity" (Prov. 17:17). Friends don't desert you when the circumstances change, or cave in when there are

[1]From *Friends for the Journey* by Madeleine L'Engle and Luci Shaw. © 1997 by Luci Shaw and Madeleine L'Engle. Published by Servant Publications, Box 8617, Ann Arbor, Michigan, 48107. Used by permission.

problems (yours, theirs, or between you). On the contrary, a real friendship kicks into high gear when there is big trouble.

A friend does not "kiss up" to you. In fact, a real friend loves you
enough to tell you the truth even if it means risking your friendship.
But beware of the flatterer, the person who tells you you're great, agrees
with all your opinions, and praises all your courses of action. That person wants something! And he or she is no friend. It is always better to
choose an honest critic than a manipulating complimenter who seems
to want to meet your every need. As Proverbs puts it, "Wounds from a
friend can be trusted, but an enemy multiplies kisses" (Prov. 27:6). A
friend loves you before, during, and after you're "somebody."

A friend is a healer. Being around a true friend is like rubbing your
chapped hands with fine cream, or as I like to say, a friend is Lancôme
for the soul! Proverbs 27:9 says, "Just as lotions and fragrance give sen-
sual delight, a sweet friendship refreshes the soul" (MESSAGE). A friend
causes you to grow as a person, as a Christian, and as a citizen. A real
friend will expand your eternal perspective and cause you to notice and
love the enduring things of life.

A great friend sees you through the hard times but doesn't leave you
there. He or she will encourage you to go on to the good things, the true
things, the lasting things. Paul was that kind of friend when he wrote,

Summing it all up, friends, I'd say you'll do best by filling your minds and meditating on things true, noble, reputable, authentic, compelling, gracious — the best, not the worst; the beautiful, not the ugly; things to praise, not things to curse.... Do that, and God, who makes everything work together, will work you into his most excellent harmonies.

PHILIPPIANS 4:8 MESSAGE

Finally, it is good to remember that even the best human friends fail. But there is a Friend who will never let you down, will never shade the truth, will never desert you when the going gets tough. This Friend could have chosen to call us many things — servants, subjects, underlings — because He was, after all, God, living on our turf. But (He said it Himself) He chose to call us friends! God calls us friends!

Bill and I have had a blessed life. We have loved each other. We have had the privilege of parenting three great kids. We have traveled the world over and seen some great places. We have shared some amazing experiences. But the greatest treasure of our lives is the gift of some wonderful, true, honest, long-term friends and the joy of walking through this life hand in hand with the One who chose to call Bill and Gloria Gaither *His* friends.

Thank You, Lord, for friends.
Through the passages of life, good friends walk with us.
    Through beauty and vitality,
       through the loss of energy and elasticity,
       through stellar achievement
            and through embarrassing failure — friends remain.
Friends give when there is need —
They celebrate and enjoy with us
    when there is abundance.
They laugh at our jokes and our foibles.
They cry at our griefs and at our sadnesses.
Friends pick up the pieces we leave,
    they take up the slack when we're careless
      and they make up the difference when we come up short.
They listen when we tell them something . . .
    and they hear when we don't.
They love our kids, tolerate our dogs, and accept our spouses.
Lord, of all the sweet relationships of earth,
    thank You for the gift of a few good friends.
And, most of all, thank You for choosing to be One to us
    who were and are so in need of one True Friend.[2]

---

[2]"Psalms and Prayers for the New Millennium." Written by Gloria Gaither. © Copyright 2000 by Gloria Gaither. All rights reserved.

I Know Where I Am Now

They loaded him in and drove to the Opry;
He was old, now, and weary and very near blind.
They pulled in the alley that led to the stage door;
They'd granted his last wish, just to be kind.

Many the time he had stood by the curtain,
Waiting his turn to walk out on the stage.
Thund'rous applause once welcomed the entrance
Of this old performer now crippled with age.

> Don't worry 'bout me; I know where I am.
> Thanks for the hand, but now I can stand.
> I'll walk on alone —
> The voices and faces — I know them all well, now
> I can hear; I can see — don't worry 'bout me —
> I'm finally home!

In life's traveling road show, I've been a performer,
When burdens were heavy, when days were too long.
When there was a part for an old country singer,
When folks needed hope, I sang them my song.

One of these days Someone will lead me
Through heaven's stage door and into the wings.
There'll be a place in that final performance —
I know my part, and I'm ready to sing.

> Don't worry 'bout me; I know where I am.
> Thanks for the hand, but now I can stand.
> I'll walk on alone —
> The faces of loved ones, the voice of my Father
> I hear and I see — don't worry 'bout me —
> I'm finally Home!

I Know Where I Am Now

~

The story is told that Roy Acuff, legendary star of country music, asked his friends to take him back to the old Ryman Auditorium one last time before he died. He was old and very nearly blind.

The Ryman had been abandoned when the beautiful Opryland auditorium was built to be the new home of *The Grand Ole Opry*. Mr. Acuff had performed to sellout crowds in the new facility, but his heart remained at the Ryman, where so many struggling artists had gotten their start and then had risen to fame. If Nashville, the Music City, were a play, the Ryman itself would be a leading character. It had been built as a revival tabernacle by a converted riverboat captain, Thomas Ryman, in honor of preacher Sam Jones, who had been used by God to turn his life around. For many years, it housed revival crusades, then it came eventually to house the premier country music live show called *The Grand Ole Opry,* which was radio broadcast nationwide by WSM in Nashville.

Who over fifty doesn't remember sitting with their family or grandparents in front of the console radio on Saturday nights, straining to hear through the static Hank Williams, Little Jimmy Dickens, Hank Snow, Red Folly, or Minnie Pearl saying "How-dee!"?

There was no real backstage area at the converted revival house. There was, however, a generous alley that ran along the side of the building onto which the stage door — such as it was — opened. There, winter and summer, the artists and singers who had been invited to sing would "hang out" until their turn came to perform. Gradually, the small print shops that lined the alley were replaced by coffee shops and bars where stargazers and artists alike would gather out of the weather to wait. Because of the famous names found there on Saturday nights, Printers' Alley soon became almost as famous a landmark as the Ryman itself.

And so it was that some of Roy Acuff's friends granted his last request and drove him in their comfortable automobile up Printers' Alley to the stage door. They helped the old gentleman out and led him up

197 · *I Know Where I Am Now* ⟩⟩

the two or three steps of the tiny stoop, through the stage door, and to the wooden homemade ramp that leads to the stage area itself. As soon as Mr. Acuff got his hand on the worn railing that runs along the ramp, he turned to his friends and said, "I'm all right now; I know where I am." Then he straightened, squared his shoulders, and walked onto the stage before the empty auditorium . . . alone.

It's anybody's guess what went on in the old man's mind as he made one last journey to center stage. His performance that night was in his memory, but one thing was sure: he had come home. His friends could see it on his face.

When Bill and I heard this story, we couldn't help recognizing it as a metaphor for us all for the song of life each of us is singing. And we couldn't help writing the song with a longtime gospel singer in mind—our friend, Jake Hess. Since then, Jake has shared this song with audiences across the country both in concerts and on video. It has reminded us that, as Shakespeare said, "All the world's a stage, and all the men and women merely players."

How well we sing our song here, how clearly we tune in to the eternal music of the Spirit, will determine how at peace we will be with the song of heaven. While we are here, if we move to the rhythm and the tempo, learn the words and the music, show up for every chance to share the song no matter how small the audience, we will find that our performance there will be natural and beautiful.

I'm Almost Home

The Savior's presence seems so dear,
Each step I take brings heaven near;
And there is nothing to hold me here,
Praise God, I'm almost home!

> I can almost see my Savior smiling,
> I can almost see Him on His throne;
> The way grows clearer,
> And heaven seems nearer,
> Praise God, I'm almost home!

What joy it is to walk this way,
My Savior calls, I cannot stay;
I see the dawn of a glorious day,
Praise God, I'm almost home!

> I can almost see my Savior smiling,
> I can almost see Him on His throne;
> The way grows clearer,
> And heaven is nearer,
> Praise God, I'm almost home!

I'm Almost Home

~

Bill and I have been very fortunate to have had many old saints in our lives who modeled what it means to follow Jesus over the years and to be faithful to our calling and commitment. One of these mentors was Bill's great uncle Jesse.

Jesse Gaither was a constant in Bill's life. He was a pray-er, a tither, and an encourager. He supported the pastor, was regular in his church attendance, and seldom criticized, even if he didn't agree with a policy or a vote on a certain issue.

Hardly an opportunity for testimonies passed without Jesse standing to tell with humor and with tears some incident from his daily life that proved God's faithfulness. He loved the Living Word of God, and he liked most people.

All the Gaither Boys — as Grandpa Gaither and his four brothers are still called — loved to laugh. They were great storytellers, and even stories they had told and heard dozens of times would make them laugh so hard the tears would roll down their cheeks. I remember the night before Bill's grandfather died, the "boys" were telling stories in our back yard and laughing so hard I could hear them in the house. The next afternoon, Grover "died with his boots on," doing the fall plowing. A kid from the neighborhood who had come to get a free haircut found him in the furrow he had just plowed.

Bill and I would sometimes take baby Suzanne over to Uncle Jesse and Aunt Hazel's house. Their living room was a quaint and quiet sort of room dominated by a large grandfather clock. The ticking of that clock seemed to emphasize that the moments we spent there were passing and that whatever we glean from them was very precious. One evening as we talked and I rocked Suzanne, Uncle Jesse said, "You know, I am coming to understand what the old saints meant when they talked about being homesick for heaven. After you live long enough, you begin to feel the scale of your life tip, and you realize you've sent on ahead more than you have left here."

He batted his eyes, a tic that endeared him to us. "Bill, sometimes it seems I can almost see the Savior smiling. Sometimes I can almost see Him on His throne."

Bill and I looked at each other, thinking the same thought, *Write that one down for a song!*

When we got home that night, we talked about what Uncle Jesse had said. Although we were a young couple just beginning our family, people like Uncle Jesse, Bill's Grandpa Grover, my Grandma Sickal, and the saints we'd both known growing up in our small town churches gave us perspective on the choices we were making and the roads we were taking.

A few mornings later, Bill and I put Uncle Jesse's words into a song that almost three decades later we are only beginning to comprehend. Although we feel we have many miles left to our journey, we find that we have sent quite a bit on ahead, and we know that it won't be long before the scale will start to tip for us. There are times when we feel a strange pang of loneliness that can only be described as homesickness for a homeland where we've made some major investments.

Resurrection

Hang out the banners and shout the news!
Blow the trumpets and horns!
'Till there is no one who has not heard:
"We shall not die anymore!"

I'm here to tell you that Jesus lives;
As He lives, so shall we!
Dying and fear have passed away,
Swallowed in victory!

> Morning has broken the cords away!
> There's no reason to fear.
> Why seek the living among the dead?
> Jesus, your Lord is not here —
> He is alive; He's not here!

Where, death, is your victory?
Where, oh grave, is your sting?
Come, children, and dance with me!
Sing to our living King!

Love wins over everything,
Melts the spears and the swords.
Join hands, let your voices ring;
Christ is our risen Lord.

> Open the prisons and ring the bells!
> Join the ransomed and free
> In celebration for what He's done;
> Jesus, the Christ sets you free —
> Jesus, the Christ sets you free!

Resurrection

It was Good Friday, and Sunday would be Easter. Death and resurrection danced together, not only in the death and resurrection of our Lord but in spring's final battle with winter. Alphas and Omegas, beginnings and endings seemed to whirl and clash in such a blinding confusion it was hard to tell them apart.

There is struggle in both dying and birthing, and although we tend to think something has to be born to die, the truth is, says the Word of the Lord, something has to die to be born. "Unless a grain of wheat falls into the earth and dies, it remains by itself alone; but if it dies, it bears much fruit" (John 12:24 NASB).

On Good Friday a year before, our daughter Suzanne was having a very difficult time with a pregnancy that had begun just two weeks before she had undergone what turned out to be major surgery. Not knowing that she had conceived, the doctor had laser-stripped her reproductive organs of a serious case of endometriosis. The hope was that this procedure would give her a chance to conceive. The truth was, a tiny life was developing already.

As the pregnancy progressed and her lasered-raw womb expanded, Suzanne grew weaker and weaker until about all she could do was sit with me on our front porch or make a short trip to the grocery store. There were times she felt she wouldn't live to mother her child; other times she was able to gain fresh energy from the hope that once the baby came, her body could begin to repair.

Then, too, she was concerned that her child might have been damaged by the surgery itself or the anesthesia she had been given.

At last, in August, little Will was born. What joy we felt, what relief, to find that he was healthy and that Suzanne had survived this whole process. Maybe that was why Bill and I were such crazy — and thankful — grandparents!

The following spring, as we enjoyed this new life given to our family and as new life sprouted all around us in nature, my mother was in the last stages of cancer. For five weeks my sister and I stayed at the hospital to be with her. "Well, we've never done *this* before," Mother said to me, for she was always an adventurer. This was the last and most risky adventure any of us had ever taken.

On that Friday before Easter, as my sister and I watched our grand-babies play games in the hospital room, our mother began her last journey. It was a difficult trip. Earth does not give up easily, and winter sometimes rages its final grasping storms violently. I remember years when there was snow even on Easter. But winter is doomed, nonetheless. Spring does come.

The blustering wind rattled the hospital windows behind the spring daffodils and hyacinths friends had sent to bring color and fragrance to Mother's room. Along the street outside, the ornamental crab trees ventured their first white and pink blossoms.

I turned from the window to rearrange the pillows to make Mother more comfortable, then leaned down to kiss the velvet cheek that was so familiar to me. Because her kidneys had almost ceased their function, her skin had turned the color of the daffodils on the windowsill. I soaked a washcloth in warm water and steamed her calloused feet, then rubbed them with expensive cream. Touch becomes very important when touch is all you have left to nurture the spirit.

This body is like the casing of a seed, I thought. *It won't be long until it will burst with the life that swells inside.* My mother had always been hungry to learn, thirsty to drink every drop of truth life could teach her. This body wouldn't hold this sprout much longer. Winter's shell would soon explode with the urgency of life.

"Death is swallowed up in victory" (1 Cor. 15:54 KJV).

Alphas—beginnings. Omegas—endings. In Him they are both the same. I had watched Will playing with his cousins, so new, so eager to learn all the new things. Mother had celebrated her eighty-fourth birthday, frustrated by the same limitations that frustrated little Will. So much to embrace, so little time.

I sat down beside my dying mother. Time and earth were shackles to her that Will was only beginning to know. Like a snake's skin, like the casing of a seed, the confines would have to give way to life.

I wrote in my journal:

The process—this alpha-omega dance, this rite of spring—may thrash and rage and threaten; but death, though it will have its ugly moment, will itself die. It's been Friday all day. Tomorrow will be Saturday. But Sunday's coming! There is Easter in our bones!

A few days later I held my mother in my arms as she breathed her last breath. A lyric I had written years before sang to my heart. I had proven it true for myself.

Where, death is your victory?
Where, O grave is your sting?
Come, children, and dance with me!
Sing to our living King!

I know Mother was dancing, too. Alleluia!

More Than Ever

It was one thing to pledge Him your heart and your soul
In the reckless, wild passions of youth;
It was easy to say that you'd go all the way
In your innocent longing for truth;
But as dreams seemed to fade and as choices were made
That took you through rugged terrain;
When you stumbled and failed and your life was assailed,
Did you ever blame God for your pain?

> Now, more than ever, I cherish the cross;
> More than ever I sit at His feet —
> All the miles of my journey have proved my Lord true —
> And He is so precious to me.

When I started my journey in fresh, childlike trust,
I believed that the Lord's way was best;
I would read in His Word how He mothered the bird
And grieved when it fell from its nest;
How I felt His delight when I chose to do right,
And I prayed I would not make Him sad;
We would meet on the way in the cool of the day;
What a pure, sweet communion we had!

> Oh, but now, more than ever, I cherish the cross;
> More than ever I sit at His feet —
> All the miles of my journey have proved my Lord true —
> And He is so precious to me.

The road I have traveled has sometimes been steep
Through wild, jagged places of life;
Sometimes I have stumbled and fallen so hard
That the stones cut my soul like a knife;

But the staff of my Shepherd would reach out for me,
And lift me to cool pastures green;
With oil of the Spirit anointing my wounds,
There I'd rest by the clear healing stream.

    So now, more than ever, I cherish the cross;
    More than ever I sit at His feet —
    All the miles of my journey have proved my Lord true —
    And He is so precious to me.

Is Love's Old Sweet Story too good to be true?
Do you find all this hard to believe?
Has the cruel world we live in so battered your heart
That the hurt child inside you can't grieve?
Oh, I can't say I blame you; I've been where you are;
But all I can say is, "It's true!"
You're wanted; you're precious, the love of His heart;
And the old rugged cross was for you.

More Than Ever

Living, as we do, in an area surrounded by Christian colleges, we often get interns at our church who are required to get some field experience before they receive their accreditation and move out to minister to the world. Most of these kids are sincere and earnest. They have studied textbooks and taken their share of exams. Several have had at least one spring-break trip to Haiti or the inner city of Chicago to do some kind of service mixed with a bout of romantic involvement with a fellow servant or two.

When they come to apprentice at our church, they shadow one of our pastoral staff and gradually take on some real responsibilities. In a few weeks they usually work themselves into leading a prayer meeting or sharing the "stewardship thought" and blessing the offering on Sunday morning. Eventually, the pastor may actually have the intern speak one Sunday night.

I am always reminded of the episode of *The Waltons* in which Grandma Walton coaches one of the boys on the fine art of preaching. She says, "Jim Bob, you need to be more forceful to emphasize your point." At that she gives their makeshift pulpit a sharp rap, then pulls back her hand in pain. "I know there's got to be a knack to it!" she says.

Some of the interns try the pulpit-pounding thing. Others practice roaming around the platform with no pulpit at all. Some hide behind the pulpit like they're afraid their fly is unzipped. Mostly these young people say true things, but not with much authority. Many of their statements begin with, "You ought to . . ." or, "They should have . . ." The old saints smile politely and nod encouragingly, while at the same time kindly tolerating a swipe or two at "the church" and at "those who call themselves Christians."

I try not to remember what I said to those much older and wiser when I was a twenty-year-old senior in college. Yet looking back, I know that I was as sincere as I knew how to be and that I longed more than anything to serve God and somehow change the world.

Bill and I used to talk for hours about our dreams and hopes. Sometimes we discussed ways we thought churches could be more effective. Now, I wonder whom we offended with our novice zeal and eager energy. Some of the things we thought would work better, have. Some of our other theories and aspirations took quite a beating in the crucible of life.

Certainly if you had told us what we were in for when we started on our journey together, we would have been scared to death! Yet we never could have imagined the amazing adventures into which God was leading us. The principles we recited back then have since been tested by the fires of real life and have proven themselves truer than we ever dreamed.

We long ago gave up trying to pound the pulpit. We found that it not only hurts the fist but also crushes the spirit. And we've found that the Holy Spirit really can be trusted to do what He does without our help. He alone can effectively convict, rebuke, teach, guide, and discipline. We only need to be faithful in prayer, constant in love, hasty in forgiveness, generous in mercy, and joyful in hope.

The cross that was an icon of our faith has become for us the cherished payment for our freedom. The blood that was a necessary but painful symbol of our salvation has become a potent and impenetrable covering we can freely apply to our relationships, our circumstances, and even our uncharted future. The blood of Jesus we now, more than ever, respect, revere, and adore.

Prayer that we once worked so hard to learn as a discipline has become as natural and as necessary as breathing. More and more, we have traded requests and demands for relationship. We are learning to ask God if we can be a part of what *He's* up to instead of expecting Him to bless what we're up to. We think of prayer these days not as a posture but as a privilege. And as living prayer has become a way of life, we have traded "how to's" for "why not's"!

We probably have fewer answers now than we used to, and most days, we have a lot more questions. But when interns come to our church, we can sure smile and nod and tell them to "preach it, sister, preach it!"

Credits

The following lyrics are reprinted with permission of the copyright holders:

"Come Sunday" — Words by Gloria Gaither. Music by William J. Gaither. © Copyright 1997 Gaither Music Company. All rights reserved. Used by permission.

"Dream On" — Words by Gloria Gaither. Music by William J. Gaither and David Huntsinger. © Copyright 1984 Gaither Music Company and Songs of Promise. All rights reserved. Used by permission.

"Even So, Lord Jesus, Come" — Words by William J. and Gloria Gaither. Music by William J. Gaither. © Copyright 1964 William J. Gaither. All rights reserved. Used by permission.

"Feeling at Home in the Presence of Jesus" — Words by William J. and Gloria Gaither. Music by William J. Gaither. © Copyright 1975 Gaither Music Company. All rights reserved. Used by permission.

"Get All Excited" — Words and music by William J. Gaither. © Copyright 1972 William J. Gaither. All rights reserved. Used by permission.

"God Gave the Song" — Words and music by Gloria Gaither, William J. Gaither, and Ronn Huff. Music by William J. Gaither and Ronn Huff. © Copyright

Other Resources by Gloria Gaither

Hardcover 0-310-21310-X

Friends Through Thick and Thin
Hardcover 0-310-22913-8

Confessions of Four Thick and Thin Friends
Hardcover 0-310-23628-2

Coming February 2001

Pick up a copy today at your local bookstore!